Classroom Go-To Guides

The Common Core in Grades 4–6: Top Nonfiction Titles from School Library Journal *and* The Horn Book Magazine, edited by Roger Sutton and Daryl Grabarek, 2014.

The Common Core in Grades 4–6

The Common Core in Grades 4–6

Top Nonfiction Titles from *School Library Journal* and *The Horn Book Magazine*

Edited by
Roger Sutton
Daryl Grabarek

ROWMAN & LITTLEFIELD
Lanham • Boulder • New York • Toronto • Plymouth, UK

Published by Rowman & Littlefield
4501 Forbes Boulevard, Suite 200, Lanham, Maryland 20706
www.rowman.com

10 Thornbury Road, Plymouth PL6 7PP, United Kingdom

British Library Cataloguing in Publication Information Available

Library of Congress Cataloging-in-Publication Data

Library of Congress Control Number: 2014934968

♻™ The paper used in this publication meets the minimum
requirements of American National Standard for Information
Sciences—Permanence of Paper for Printed Library Materials,
ANSI/NISO Z39.48-1992.

Printed in the United States of America

Contents

Preface

THE COMMON CORE IN GRADES 4–6 is the first in a series of comprehensive tools to tap into the vast flow of recently published books for children and teens, offering recommendations of exemplary titles for use in the classroom. Currency meets authority, brought to you by the editors of the highly regarded review sources *School Library Journal* and *The Horn Book Magazine*.

This guide includes approximately 200 selections published since 2007 for grades 4-6 recommended by *The Horn Book Magazine*. The titles are grouped by subject and complemented by *School Library Journal's* "Focus On" columns, which spotlight specific topics across the curriculum. Providing context for the guide, and suggestions on how to use these resources within a standards framework, is an introduction by Common Core experts Mary Ann Cappiello and Myra Zarnowski. These educators provide perspective on the key changes brought by the new standards, including suggestions on designing lessons and two sample plans.

Following the introduction, you'll find a wealth of books, by category. (Note that the guide is Dewey-Decimal based, so you may want to dig around, for example, in "Business & Technology" to find some titles that you might first seek in "World History" or "Science.") Each section includes a listing of the top titles with brief, explicit annotations, and key bibliographic data. "Focus On" articles are appended to appropriate categories to support in-depth curricular development. Each of these articles includes a topic overview and list of current and retrospective resources (including some fiction) and multimedia, enabling educators to respond to the Common Core State Standards call to work across formats.

We hope you find this guide useful, and we welcome any feedback.

— *The Editors*

Introduction

Putting Nonfiction to Work in Schools:

The Challenges and Opportunities of Implementing CCSS

Mary Ann Cappiello, Ed.D., *Lesley University*
Myra Zarnowski, Ed.D., *Queens College, CUNY*

SCHOOL CURRICULUM today is in a state of flux. Educators are asking and searching for answers to three persistent questions: What do I teach? How do I teach it? What materials do I use? The Common Core State Standards [CCSS], the major force behind current curriculum changes, require significant shifts in our methodologies.

In a nutshell, the CCSS are asking us to:

Introduce more nonfiction across the curriculum

Include more reading and writing to inform, persuade, and convey experience.

Introduce students to increasing levels of text complexity

Focus on text-based evidence when reading, writing, and speaking

Incorporate academic vocabulary in all curriculum areas

These shifts require us to revise our approach to teaching. To begin, we need to identify nonfiction titles that provide a foundation for learning. Quite simply, we need thought-provoking, imaginative, and well- written and illustrated books and materials—"stuff" that's good to think with. Fortunately, that material is currently available, and this resource will guide you to it. As we work with quality nonfiction and think deeply about it, we can also engage in activities that meet the CCSS.

It's that straightforward. We'll also have the opportunity to delve into stimulating topics and think about social issues. That's where the true pleasure of teaching and learning resides—not in overdoses of test preparation.

The resources identified by *School Library Journal* and *The Horn Book Guide* can help us meet the standards, whether they are the CCSS or standards in science, social studies, mathematics, or the language arts. These publications have already identified outstanding literature that supports our work. *School Library Journal*—the world's largest reviewer of books, multimedia, and technology for children and teens—evaluates books in terms of literary quality, artistic merit, clarity of presentation, and appeal to the intended audience. Its reviews also make connections between new and existing titles, a valuable aid in finding texts to compare features or points of view. *The Horn Book* Guide's semi-annual issue reviews more than 2,000 titles—nearly every children's title published in the United States over a six-month period. Between 1989 and 2013 alone it has published 91,920 reviews. Drawing from these outstanding resources, this "Go-To Guide" identifies the best nonfiction books available for grades four through six that will allow educators to build a content-rich foundation for teaching and learning. Here is the answer to the question, What materials do I use?

What do I need to know about nonfiction trade books?

The requirement that elementary school students read 50 percent informational text and 50 percent literature is an important component of any school's curricular transition to the CCSS. While much energy is focused on aligning methodologies and assessments to the standards, it's also important for everyone who works with students, including administrators, teachers, librarians, and classroom aides, to have an understanding of the kinds of nonfiction picture and chapter books that have emerged during the past decade. The success of any curricular unit is dependent on the quality of the materials used and the level of engagement that those materials and carefully designed classroom activities and assignments offer students. Now more than ever, books to match your students' interests and your teaching needs are available. What do you need to know about these trade titles to make appropriate selections for your classroom?

The medium and the message

Like so much else in our world, nonfiction books have become highly visual. Gone are the occasional photographs that might punctuate a volume. Brightly colored photographs, archival images, and artwork in every conceivable medium illustrate today's offerings, providing students with an opportunity to think about content through both word and image. Carefully placed pictures in chapter books carry a narrative thread of their own, much like the images in a picture book. From the cover illustration to the color or pattern of the interior and end pages, layout and design also contribute to a book's meaning; consider Steve Jenkins's signature cut-paper collage, Kadir Nelson's oil paintings, Nic Bishop's color photography, or the mixed-media collage styles of Bryan Collier and Melissa Sweet. It's important for us to model for our students how to read images, and to discuss with them the different roles illustrations can serve in conveying information and establishing theme.

Picture books for older elementary students

You might also be surprised to discover the range of nonfiction picture books available for children ages 8 to 12. While this age group is capable of reading lengthier volumes, a picture book's brevity allows for the introduction of sophisticated concepts and ideas in manageable doses. Nonfiction picture books can also model a range of styles and structures during writing instruction. However, it's important to note that not all titles are effective as read alouds. Some are, some aren't; the more you read, the easier it will be to determine those titles that are best for small group or individual reading and those that can be read aloud to a large group.

The range of nonfiction

In addition to finding a variety of picture and chapter books in this guide, you'll also marvel at the range of topics, genres, and approaches. Students unfamiliar with nonfiction texts may assume that every nonfiction title serves the same function. This is not the case. Having an understanding of what those purposes are can help students understand why an author selected a particular structure for a book, and how the two work together to create meaning. Surveys, concept books, biographies and autobiographies, specialized nonfiction, and resources such as almanacs, atlases, field guides, and how-to titles also employ an array of arrangements and styles from narrative, exposition, question and answer, compare and contrast, or problem/solution.

On any given topic, teachers might find several books that feature different perspectives. For example, in this guide you'll discover Caroline Arnold's *Global Warming and the Dinosaurs: Fossil Discoveries at the Poles*, an overview of the dinosaurs that inhabited the polar regions during the Cretaceous Period, and a survey of prehistoric marine reptiles in her *Giant Sea Reptiles of the Dinosaur Age*, while Deborah Kogan Ray's *Dinosaur Mountain: Digging Into the Jurassic Period* focuses on fossil hunter Earl Douglas and early dinosaur research in the United States.

Knowing about the range of books available allows you to incorporate the varied perspectives students are asked to consider in the CCSS.

Visible authors

Nonfiction authors often speak directly to their readers about researching, writing, and interpreting factual information. Their notes are excellent resources. Sharing authors' comments with children will help them begin to understand how writers sift and shape information and question the facts they uncover.

Each of the books listed below includes a note in which the author discusses his or her work with readers. Their reflections highlight different aspects of reading and writing nonfiction. Examples of the aspects covered are given below.

Life in the Ocean: The Story of Oceanographer Sylvia Earle by **Claire A. Nivola**. In this picture book biography, Nivola discusses various interpretations of Earle's life and suggests how she believes her life should be understood. After reading this note, you can begin a conversation on multiple perspectives or, in this case, different ways to understand a life story.

Barnum's Bones: How Barnum Brown Discovered the Most Famous Dinosaur in the World by **Tracey Fern**. Fern comments that Barnum Brown, dinosaur hunter and fossil finder, did not keep detailed field notes or routinely publish reports of his scientific discoveries. This is a useful opening when considering how biographers and historians deal with gaps in available information.

Marching for Freedom: Walk Together, Children, and Don't You Grow Weary by **Elizabeth Partridge**. Partridge explains to readers how seeing photos of the Selma-Montgomery march sparked her interest in researching and writing about the role of children in the historic event. Using this example, discuss the question authors are often asked: How do you get your ideas for writing?

Trapped: How the World Rescued 33 Miners from 2,000 Feet Below the Chilean Desert by **Marc Aronson**. In a section entitled "How I Wrote This Book and What I Learned That Could be Useful for Students Writing Research Reports (and a Couple of Last Thoughts from Men I Interviewed)," Aronson describes how, in writing about a current event, he had to rely on the Internet for much of his information. He describes some strategies for using the Internet to dig deeply into a topic, strategies that can be shared with students.

Nonfiction trade books are essential sources for learning about content and process. In addition to writers' comments, author interviews and websites often provide more information about the writing process.

Nonfiction across the curriculum in grades 4-6: What to teach? How?

Since nonfiction literature fuels the curriculum, selecting books that introduce new content and stimulate thinking is essential to planning. But there is more. Constructing curriculum involves merging three distinct pieces: standards, nonfiction, and hands-on activities.

Incorporating all three of these aspects into a unit can be difficult, but it also allows us to be creative. In reality, we have no choice since the CCSS does not offer specific curriculum. Planning is a challenging yet rewarding job because it allows librarians and educators to make important decisions about teaching and learning. Below is a brief sample of how this works in the language arts and the sciences.

Language arts

There are many options for including more nonfiction within the traditional domain of the language arts. By the time students reach fourth grade, they are reading independently, having mastered, by and large, the art of decoding. However, we grow ever more sophisticated as readers when we read with a particular purpose in mind. These purposes are limitless, and can be established by the teacher or the student. Students' interests and goals may guide their independent reading life and lead them toward reading ever more sophisticated texts. Teachers have particular standards-based reading behaviors they need to model and practice in guided reading groups.

One example of how to design a curriculum in language arts is to think about how theme is established in a text. Understanding that students learn best when they are reading and writing with the same focus, a writing workshop curriculum for fifth grade (incorporating fiction and nonfiction) could be implemented around the notion of theme. Students would read a selection of books, then write their own original pieces modeled on those they have read.

Standards: This particular curriculum unit could draw upon CCSS for reading literature and informational text. Using the standards listed below, design curriculum that asks students to read fiction from the same genre (short stories, novels, fables, or folktales), or a combination of them, and then a combination of nonfiction texts (picture book or chapter books).

CCSS.ELA-Literacy.RL.5.2 Determine a theme of a story, drama, or poem from details in the text, including how characters in a story or drama respond to challenges or how the speaker in a poem reflects upon a topic; summarize the text.

CCSS.ELA-Literacy.RL.5.9 Compare and contrast stories in the same genre (e.g., mysteries and adventure stories) on their approaches to similar themes and topics.

CCSS.ELA-Literacy.RI.5.1 Quote accurately from a text when explaining what the text says explicitly and when drawing inferences from the text.

CCSS.ELA-Literacy.RI.5.6 Analyze multiple accounts of the same event or topic, noting important similarities and differences in the point of view they represent.

Of course, state and local standards for social studies and science can also be used to select nonfiction titles that convey a theme and meet content standards.

Once students complete their reading, they can begin their own original compositions that establish a theme, focusing on the following standard: "CCSS.ELA-Literacy. W.5.3 Write narratives to develop real or imagined experiences or events using effective technique, descriptive details, and clear event sequences is identified."

Nonfiction: You probably already use a great deal of fiction in your language arts curriculum and reading and writing workshop to choose from for this particular unit. There may also be some nonfiction titles that are ideally suited to this task, but be aware that not every nonfiction title will be. Examining texts with this in mind will make your selection more precise than selecting works solely on broad content.

Many of the books included in this guide are ideally suited for an exploration of theme in nonfiction. For example, some of your students could read Elaine Scott's *When is a Planet Not a Planet? The Story of Pluto*, while others might delve into HP Newquist's *Here There Be Monsters: The Legendary Kraken and the Giant Squid*. While these titles address different topics, they share the view that science is a work in progress. Not only do scientists not agree on the very definition of a planet, but they are discovering new information that challenges the ways in which "planet" has been defined in the past. Similarly, the giant squid was once the stuff of legend; only now are we learning about this mysterious creature, and our understanding continues to grow and change. Of course, another approach might be to examine nonfiction texts on the same topic and examine the different themes that emerge.

Hands-On Activities: Ideally, starting with a read aloud that compares and contrasts two texts will provide your students with a model to do the same. As students make their way through a range of titles independently or in groups, you'll want to find a way for them to document the ideas they see at work and the evidence they discover. Forms for note taking and some larger, poster-size documentation should be made available so that the thinking is visible. Short clips of television and radio advertisements are a concrete way of introducing theme in a familiar format to students. Following other typical writing workshop procedures, students will be constructing their own texts, based on "real or imagined experiences," that incorporate a particular idea.

Science

To put the pieces together in science and design a living curriculum, it's necessary to consider standards, nonfiction, and hands-on activities. Here's one example of how this works when teaching intermediate grade science on the topic of Earth systems.

Standards: The standards to consider are The Next Generation Science Standards, which can be found at http://www.nextgenscience.org/next-generation-science-standards and Common Core State Standards for reading, writing, and discussing informational text at http://www.corestandards.org/ELA-Literacy

Beginning with the science standards, we find that in the intermediate grades, students are expected to learn about ways individual communities use science ideas to protect the Earth's resources and environment (5-ESS3-1). The science standards also provide relevant connections to CCSS, noting that students should able to explain ideas by drawing on multiple resources, quoting accurately from books and materials, summarizing information, and support analysis, reflection, and research (RI.5.1, RI.5.7, RI.5.9, W.5.8, W.5.9). With these ideas in mind, we can locate the nonfiction titles we want to use.

Nonfiction: Two books that would support an inquiry into protecting our planet's resources and environment are Sandra Markle's *The Case of the Vanishing Golden Frogs* and Marty Crump's *The Mystery of Darwin's Frog*.

The Case of the Vanishing Golden Frogs describes how the biologist Karen Lips returned to Fortuna Forest Reserve in Panama after a four-year absence to learn that the Panamanian gold frog population—once healthy and thriving—was dying out. Figuring out why the frogs are vanishing is at the center of this mystery that eventually becomes an international cause. One of several theories suggested is the fungus Bd. Readers learn how careful observation and creative thinking are necessary aspects of a scientific investigation.

The Mystery of Darwin's Frog describes a frog discovered by the naturalist Charles Darwin during his travels and later named after him. Males of this unusual species keep their young in their vocal sacs, nurturing them before they release them. While much of the book details the behavior of Darwin's frogs, scientist Marty Crump also discusses the problems that all frogs are facing—the growing threat of the Bd fungus, as well as loss of habitat and pollution. The connections to *The Case of the Vanishing Golden Frogs* are clear.

Hands-On Activities: After reading these titles, one activity might be to conduct an imaginary interview with Karen Lips or Marty Crump. Students can pose questions and provide answers about how these and other scientists are working to design a solution to the problems they are witnessing. In the process, students will learn that science involves questioning, observing, hypothesizing, testing, and collecting data and analyzing it, which often leads to more questions. Preparing interview questions will also draw on reading and writing skills.

This lesson could easily be extended by adding further resources—books, newspaper and magazine articles, DVDs, websites, photographs, and more.

Becoming Decision Makers

The new standards documents provide us with goals to meet, but not the route to meet them. By putting educators in the position of decision makers, the standards allow us to do what we do best—decide how to teach and what materials to use. Here is the opportunity to be creative while responding to the interests of our students and to select materials and design lessons around them. *The Common Core in Grades 4–6* will support us as we shape the curriculum in our classrooms and libraries.

As you and your team continue to realign your curriculum to the CCSS and consider new ways to explore the language arts, the sciences, and social studies, this guide can be turned to again and again to learn about exemplary nonfiction texts. The following questions might also help you navigate the guide:

What is the content of the curriculum standards I must teach in this particular unit?

What subheading should I go to first to find the trade books that match the content?

What are some of the subgenres of nonfiction that provide a range of approaches to the topic?

What aspects of a nonfiction book can help me to teach writing as well as science or social studies?

How does the review point me toward ways that I can use this book in the classroom for content and language arts curriculum?

Using this guide to select trade books for your curriculum puts you in the driver's seat. It's not necessary to purchase an expensive program to meet the Common Core State Standards. Adding the resources that you already have to create new curriculum units, and/or working with your school librarian to purchase text sets of books to revise existing lesson plans, you can construct engaging curriculum that will be meaningful for your students. Think about the books you already have in different ways and consider how adding a range of nonfiction books can support your work in teaching the language arts, science, and social studies.

Books cited

Arnold, C. (2007). *Giant Sea Reptiles of the Dinosaur Age*. New York: Clarion.

—(2009). *Global Warming and the Dinosaurs: Fossil Discoveries at the Poles*. New York: Clarion.

Aronson, M. (2011). *Trapped: How the World Rescued 33 Miners from 2,000 Feet Below the Chilean Desert*. New York, NY: Atheneum.

Bradley, T. J. (2008) *Paleo Bugs: Survival of the Creepiest*. San Francisco: Chronicle.

Crump, M. (2013). *The Mystery of Darwin's Frog*. Illus. S. Jenkins & E. Rodriguez. Honesdale, PA: Boyds Mills Press.

Fern, T. (2012). *Barnum's Bones: How Barnum Brown Discovered the Most Famous Dinosaur in the World*. New York, NY: Farrar, Straus, Giroux.

Markle, S. (2012). *The Case of the Vanishing Golden Frogs: A Scientific Mystery*. Minneapolis, MN: Millbrook Press.

Newquist, H.P. (2010). *Here There be Monsters: The Legendary Kraken and the Giant Squid*. Boston: Houghton Mifflin.

Nivola, C. A. (2012). *Life in the Ocean: The Story of Sylvia Earle*. New York, NY: Farrar, Straus, Giroux.

Arts

Q **Ancona, George.** Ole! Flamenco. 48 pp. Lee 2010. ISBN 978-1-60060-361-7.
Flamenco student Janira and her classmates learn an "art that goes back a long, long time." Ancona's narration skillfully paces Janira's preparation for performance with the history of flamenco, encompassing music, song, and dance, and the inextricably connected history of the Roma. Accompanying photographs capture the dancers' and musical accompanists' expressive bodies and faces mid-gesture. Bib., glos.
Performing Arts; Dance; Romany

Q **Brown, Monica.** Tito Puente: Mambo King/Rey del Mambo. 32 pp. HarperCollins/ Rayo 2013. ISBN 978-0-06-122783-7. Illustrated by Rafael López.
A bilingual picture book charts the life of Tito Puente with all the exuberance of the drummer and bandleader's irresistible music. Vibrant imagery hums right off the page, full of high-contrast color and energetic composition, and decorated with swirling, starry embellishments. The treatment is not especially deep and is decidedly positive: Tito's life reads like a sequence of successes.
Individual Biographies; Foreign languages–Spanish language; Music–Latin music; Puente, Tito; Musicians; Harlem (New York, NY); Hispanic Americans

Q **Bryan, Ashley.** Let It Shine: Three Favorite Spirituals. 48 pp. Atheneum (Simon & Schuster Children's Publishing) 2007. ISBN 978-0-689-84732-5.
Using only cut-paper and clamorous, swirling, out-of-sight colors, Bryan sets three spirituals to pictures that are dynamic, monumental, and stirring. Throughout, the imagery is brilliant. Bryan has long been known for his exuberant decorative motifs, but in this instance, with three sets of lyrics that are themselves all imagery, his scope widens. With words and music appended: exciting, absorbing, immensely moving.
Music; African Americans; Songs–Hymns; Songs–Spirituals

Q **Christensen, Bonnie.** Fabulous!: A Portrait of Andy Warhol. 40 pp. Holt/Ottaviano 2011. ISBN 978-0-8050-8753-6.
Profiling the "Prince of Pop Art" from his 1930s Pittsburgh childhood through the height of his fame in 1966, Christensen shows that Andy Warhol became a visionary artist through determination and hard work. Highly textured oil and collage illus-

trations, which incorporate "replicas" of Warhol's art, provide a solid backdrop to a life that came to seem, in later years, glitzy and unreal.

Visual Arts; Biographies; Warhol, Andy; Painting; Pop art

Close, Chuck. Chuck Close: Face Book. 56 pp. Abrams 2012. ISBN 978-1-4197-0163-4. In this Q&A–style narrative, Close answers questions supposedly asked by children. His voice is clear and direct with not a hint of famous-artist self-aggrandizement or angst. A central section shows fourteen of his self-portraits in a variety of media on heavy card stock cut into thirds so readers can mix and match. A welcome primary source about being an artist. Timeline. Bib., glos., ind.

Visual Arts; Disabilities, Learning–Dyslexia; Disabilities, Physical; Biographies; Toy and movable books; Artists; Close, Chuck

Diakité, Baba Wagué. A Gift from Childhood: Memories of an African Boyhood. 136 pp. Groundwood (House of Anansi Press) 2010. ISBN 978-0-88899-931-3 PE ISBN 978-1-55498-421-3.

Malian artist Diakité's ceramic tiles illustrate this autobiography. The medium admirably suits the subject: rural Mali comes to life in the tiles' earth tones, saturated colors, and bold drafting, supplemented with Diakité's handsome portraits and traditional designs. His story's significance shines through the simplicity of its telling; Malian village life is revealed in authentic detail, and the cultural attitudes are mind-opening.

Visual Arts; Mali; Africa; Blacks; Artists; Biographies; Autobiographies

Fleming, Candace. The Great and Only Barnum: The Tremendous, Stupendous Life of Showman P. T. Barnum. 151 pp. Random/Schwartz & Wade 2009. ISBN 978-0-375-84197-2 LE ISBN 978-0-375-94597-7. Illustrated by Ray Fenwick.

Big-top pioneer Barnum had an equally indelible effect on the history of museums and zoology. This biography captures the spirit of the man and his era. While Fleming lauds his accomplishments, she doesn't shy away from ethical issues that, from a modern perspective, threaten to tarnish his legacy. The handsome book design includes an abundance of photographs and illustrations, sidebars and subheadings. Websites. Bib., ind.

Individual Biographies; Barnum, P. T.; Circuses; Entrepreneurship

Friedman, Lise. Becoming a Ballerina: A Nutcracker Story. 48 pp. Viking 2012. ISBN 978-0-670-01392-0. Photographs by Mary Dowdle.

This photo-essay follows young Boston Ballet student Fiona as she auditions for the role of Clara in *The Nutcracker*, wins the part, and prepares for her performance. Crisp color photographs document the ballet company onstage and behind the scenes. Young dancers will be entranced by the rehearsal, costuming, and staging details; *Nutcracker* fans will treasure this intimate view of a holiday tradition.

Performing Arts; Dance–Ballet; Boston (MA)

 Golio, Gary. Spirit Seeker: John Coltrane's Musical Journey. 48 pp. Clarion 2012. ISBN 978-0-547-23994-1. Illustrated by Rudy Gutierrez.

This picture-book biography (best for older children and young teens) successfully describes Coltrane's music and what made it distinctive. The sophisticated illustrations show faces with almost photographic realism, while the lines depicting the background scenes are intentionally distorted and abstracted into swirling shapes. Thus the art ingeniously gets across the story's intangibles: Coltrane's pain, his drug-addled mind, his spirituality, and his music. Discography, reading list, website.

Individual Biographies; Coltrane, John; African Americans; Musical instruments–Saxophone; Musicians; Music–Jazz; Substance abuse

Gonyea, Mark. A Book About Color: A Clear and Simple Guide for Young Artists. 96 pp. Holt 2010. ISBN 978-0-8050-9055-0.

Gonyea's square format, generous use of space, and breezy, informal style work well with the topic. We learn about warm and cool colors, the emotional impact of colors, and the color wheel. Individual chapters and a text that covers only one simple idea per spread allow concepts to sink in. The casual tone makes new terminology and ideas seem less daunting.

Visual Arts; Color

Greenberg, Jan and Jordan, Sandra. Ballet for Martha: Making Appalachian Spring. 48 pp. Roaring Brook/Flash Point/Porter 2010. ISBN 978-1-59643-338-0. Illustrated by Brian Floca.

After choreographer Martha Graham asked composer Aaron Copland and sculptor/set designer Isamu Noguchi to collaborate with her on a new ballet, the iconic *Appalachian Spring* was born. Using spare, concise sentences, the authors echo Graham's approach to dance: nothing's wasted, and in such exactness lies beauty. Floca's fluid, energetic line and watercolor illustrations also reflect the plain boldness of Graham's choreography. Websites. Bib.

Performing Arts; Dance–Ballet; Composers; Choreographers; Graham, Martha; Women–Biographies; Biographies; Women–Choreographers; Noguchi, Isamu; Copland, Aaron; Artists

Greenberg, Jan and Jordan, Sandra. Christo and Jeanne-Claude: Through the Gates and Beyond. 50 pp. Roaring Brook/Flash Point 2008. ISBN 978-1-59643-071-6.

In addition to chronicling the evolution of *The Gates* and other pursuits, this book introduces readers to the nature of artistic vision, the role of collaboration, and the dedication of artists. The writing is lively, including many quotes from Christo and Jeanne-Claude. Crisp, vibrant photographs and detailed reproductions of Christo's drawings show both the behind-the-scenes labor and the finished projects. Bib.

Visual Arts; Artists; Jeanne-Claude; Christo; Women–Artists; Biographies; Women–Biographies; Installation art

Lang Lang, Lang Lang: Playing with Flying Keys. 221 pp. Delacorte 2008. ISBN 978-0-385-73578-0 LE ISBN 978-0-385-90564-0 PE ISBN 978-0-440-42284-6.

With Michael French. The superstar pianist chronicles his childhood and adolescence. His writing style is easygoing, but Lang Lang is also honest about the hard work and sacrifice a music career demands, in addition to being frank about his relationship with his bullying, hard-driving father. It's a compelling and enthusiastic self-portrait, accompanied by an insert of photos and list of "vital statistics." Timeline. Glos.

Individual Biographies; Lang Lang; China; Musical instruments–Piano; Music–Classical music; Family–Father and son; Autobiographies; Musicians

Losure, Mary. The Fairy Ring: Or, Elsie and Frances Fool the World. 184 pp. Candlewick 2012. ISBN 978-0-7636-5670-6.

Losure has written a well-researched and engaging account of what happened when Frances Griffiths and Elsie Wright, two young cousins in early twentieth century England, staged some photographs of fairies (reproduced here). Focusing sympathetically on the girls, the straightforward narrative goes on to report how they responded as adults when the story periodically resurfaced in the media. Bib., ind.

Individual Biographies; Women–Biographies; Children; Fairies; Family–Cousins; England;Photography; Hoaxes

J
741.6 Marcus, Leonard S. A Caldecott Celebration: Seven Artists and Their Paths to the Caldecott Medal. 55 pp. Walker 2008. ISBN 978-0-8027-9703-2 LE ISBN 978-0-8027-9704-9. New ed., 1998.

Marcus presents a gathering of essays on seven of the Caldecott honorees, one from each decade: Robert McCloskey, Marcia Brown, Maurice Sendak, William Steig, Chris Van Allsburg, David Wiesner, and, in this updated edition, Mordicai Gerstein. The text is remarkable for the smooth integration of explanatory material with overall commentary, and selective detail creates a sense of intimacy and understanding. Timeline. Glos., ind.

Visual Arts; Biographies; Illustrators; Children's literature

J
818
M Marcus, Leonard S. Pass It Down: Five Picture-Book Families Make Their Mark. 56 pp. Walker 2007. ISBN 978-0-8027-9600-4 LE ISBN 978-0-8027-9601-1.

Marcus looks at four families of picture-book artists (and one writer/artist family). He provides glimpses into their lives, leaving it to the reader to spot the similarities and differences among them. Photos of the book creators and reproductions of their work illustrate the text. The only disappointment is a truncated list of published works by each family.

Collective Biographies; Family; Illustrators; Authors; Artists; Children's literature

Mark, Jan. The Museum Book: A Guide to Strange and Wonderful Collections. 56 pp. Candlewick 2007. ISBN 978-0-7636-3370-7 PE ISBN 978-1-4063-1972-9. Illustrated by Richard Holland.

Reading this book is like wandering through an eclectic and idiosyncratic museum. Mark's conversational text ranges from where the word "museum" comes from to the ethics of displaying looted objects to the idea of memory as one's own museum. Her voice (posthumous, alas) is strong and the information far from dry and dusty. Whimsical stylized illustrations accompany the text. Glos., ind.

Visual Arts; Art appreciation; Museums

O Markel, Michelle. The Fantastic Jungles of Henri Rousseau. 40 pp. Eerdmans 2012. ISBN 978-0-8028-5364-6. Illustrated by Amanda Hall.

Markel's informative text conveys self-taught modern artist Henri Rousseau's groundbreaking flat perspective, inspiration by faraway lands, and determined personality, as well as interesting details such as his place in a circle of Modernist artists and writers. Hall's lush watercolor and acrylic art bears a clear resemblance to Rousseau's. This successful tribute makes Rousseau accessible, and inspirational, to a young audience.

Visual Arts; Rousseau, Henri; Painting; Artists; Biographies; France; Jungles; Creativity

Martin, Russell and Nibley, Lydia. The Mysteries of Beethoven's Hair. 120 pp. Charlesbridge 2009. ISBN 978-1-57091-714-1.

While paying last respects, composer-in-training Ferdinand Hiller snipped a lock of Beethoven's hair. Mysteries dogging the memento are the focus of this absorbing book (adapted from Martin's adult work *Beethoven's Hair*). The text explores Beethoven's troubled life, the modern-day quest to prove the cause of his death, and the keepsake's journey through history. Many well-captioned black-and-white art reproductions and photographs add tangibility. Ind.

Music; Human body–Hair; Beethoven, Ludwig van; Composers; Forensic science; Music–Classical music

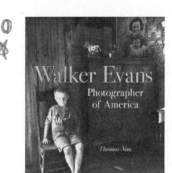

Nau, Thomas. Walker Evans: Photographer of America. 64 pp. Roaring Brook/Porter 2007. ISBN 978-1-59643-225-3. Walker Evans's innovative photographs of America from the 1930s through the 1970s recorded scenes without imposing an interpretation; similarly, Nau presents facts crisply and lucidly and asks readers to interpret them as they will, often posing questions about the photographs' subjects. While the overall structure is chronological, each chapter highlights a portion of Evans's work or his development as an artist. Source notes are included. Timeline. Bib., ind.

Visual Arts; History, American; Biographies; Photography; Evans, Walker

Nelson, Marilyn. Sweethearts of Rhythm: The Story of the Greatest All-Girl Swing Band in the World. 80 pp. Dial 2009. ISBN 978-0-8037-3187-5. Illustrated by Jerry Pinkney.

Twenty poems, voiced by instruments, summarize (somewhat obliquely) the history of swing. Nelson's verbal evocations of the music and its players, and her wry asides, re-create the time period. Pinkney's vibrant watercolors, with such additions as scraps of music, capture the players' courage, the joys of performance, the sober face of war, and the reality of segregation. Timeline, websites. Bib.

Poetry; Women–African Americans; African Americans; Bands; Music–Jazz; Musicians; Gender roles; Women–Musicians

⭐○ **Nivola, Claire A.** Orani: My Father's Village. 40 pp. Farrar/Foster 2011. ISBN 978-0-374-35657-6.

In the 1950s, Nivola's father's Sardinian birthplace, with its modest red roofs, scenic valley, and welcoming relatives, was a mind-opening place to visit. Orani and its people are lovingly evoked in watercolor and gouache paintings, from expansive views to more intimate scenes. It's not a nostalgic picture, but one of children thriving in a close-knit community nurtured by its simple way of life.

Individual Biographies; Autobiographies; Women–Autobiographies; Women–Biographies; Family–Father and daughter; Italy; City and town life

Nobleman, Marc Tyler. Boys of Steel: The Creators of Superman. 40 pp. Knopf (Random House Children's Books) 2008. ISBN 978-0-375-83802-6 LE ISBN 978-0-375-93802-3 PE ISBN 978-0-449-81063-7. Illustrated by Ross MacDonald.

Jerry Siegel imagines and writes about a hero, an alien with incredible strength whose secret identity is an ordinary guy. Jerry's look-alike friend Joe Shuster illustrates his work. MacDonald's retro images show the friends sporting matching glasses and button-down shirts, fitting right into the circa-1930s world. Nobleman's author's note continues the story and explores the business side of comics. Bib.

Individual Biographies; Siegel, Jerry; Cartoons and comics; Heroes; Shuster, Joe; Jews

○ **Rubin, Susan Goldman.** Music Was IT: Young Leonard Bernstein. 178 pp. Charlesbridge 2011. ISBN 978-1-58089-344-2.

Leonard Bernstein, through a lot of perseverance and a little luck, made his conducting debut at Carnegie Hall with the New York Philharmonic at age twenty-five. Rubin's biography, focusing on the youth and early adulthood of its subject, succeeds with her engaging style and infectious passion. Numerous black-and-white photographs appear throughout. Biographical sketches and a discography are appended. Timeline. Bib., ind.

Individual Biographies; Music–Classical music; Bernstein, Leonard; Musicians; Conductors (Music); Composers; Jews

○ **Rubin, Susan Goldman.** Wideness & Wonder: The Art and Life of Georgia O'Keeffe. 117 pp. Chronicle 2011. ISBN 978-0-8118-6983-6.

As a teen, Georgia O'Keeffe attracted attention for her nonconformist attire and unconventional behavior. Rubin describes her early life and education before discussing

O'Keeffe's big break: a show at pioneering photographer—and future husband—Arthur Stieglitz's gallery; the text gives thoughtful consideration to their partnership. Central to the book are magnificent reproductions of O'Keeffe's pictures, from student sketches to commercial work to lush-hued abstracts. Bib., ind.

Visual Arts; Biographies; Women–Artists; Artists; Women–Biographies; O'Keeffe, Georgia; Painting

○ **Say, Allen.** Drawing from Memory. 64 pp. Scholastic 2011. ISBN 978-0-545-17686-6. This rendering of Say's adolescence—a coming-of-age story within the context of a long life and vocation—takes the form of an album, with text, photographs, drawings, and paintings. At the center of the book is Say's relationship with Noro Shinpei, a popular cartoonist who took Say on as an apprentice at thirteen. Throughout the volume, content is reinforced through canny artistic choices and harmonious design.

Visual Arts; Children's literature; Illustrators; Artists; Biographies; Say, Allen; Drawing; Autobiographies; Japan; Japanese Americans

○ **Schubert, Leda.** Monsieur Marceau. 40 pp. Roaring Brook/
Porter 2012. ISBN 978-1-59643-529-2. Illustrated
by Gérard DuBois.

In this biography of Marcel Marceau (alter-ego, mime Bip), declarative sentences artfully capture the performer's essence. The emphasis is on Marceau as an artist, but Schubert doesn't shy away from his persecution as a Jew during the Holocaust. DuBois's vigorous illustrations strikingly cast Marceau as a mostly white figure against black backgrounds. An afterword and miming tips are appended. Reading list.

Individual Biographies; Performing arts; Jews; History, Modern–Holocaust; France; Marceau, Marcel; Mimes

○ **Stamaty, Mark Alan.** Shake, Rattle & Turn That Noise Down!: How Elvis Shook Up Music, Me and Mom. 40 pp. Knopf (Random House Children's Books) 2010. ISBN 978-0-375-84685-4 LE ISBN 978-0-375-94685-1.

Cartoonist Stamaty's account of how his eight-year-old self discovered rock 'n' roll is rich in character, incident, family dynamics, and period detail. Mark is driven wild by Elvis Presley's music; his mom is driven crazy. Stamaty's dough-faced grinning caricatures glow with a surprising warmth that should reach across generations to grab kids and make them think twice about their grandparents.

Music; Family–Mother and son; Music–Rock music; Presley, Elvis; Biographies; Autobiographies

○ **Young, Ed.** The House Baba Built: An Artist's Childhood in China. 48 pp. Little 2011. ISBN 978-0-316-07628-9. As told to Libby Koponen.

In 1934, Ed Young's father built a house in Shanghai's "safest part," and it became a wartime refuge for the family. Young maintains a child's-eye view, focusing on life in the house and the children's games. Collages of beautifully integrated textured materials and family photos are interwoven with hand-drawn portraits, sketches, paintings, architectural diagrams, and gatefolds. Timeline.

Visual Arts; Chinese Americans; Autobiographies; Dwellings; Young, Ed; Artists; Biographies; Children's literature; Illustrators; China; History, Modern–World War II

Business & Technology

○ **Aronson, Marc.** If Stones Could Speak: Unlocking the Secrets of Stonehenge. 64 pp. National (National Geographic Books) 2010. ISBN 978-1-4263-0599-3 LE ISBN 978-1-4263-0600-6.

Archaeologist Mike Parker Pearson and his associates embarked on a series of digs that have challenged our understanding of Stonehenge (which Pearson believes to be a sacred burial site). Aronson's prose is both clear and succinct, and he invites readers to test this new theory for themselves. A map of the region, captioned photographs, and occasional sidebars complement the text. Reading list, timeline, websites. Glos., ind.

Ancient and Medieval History; Stonehenge (England); Archaeology; England

J **Aronson, Marc.** Trapped: How the World Rescued 33 Miners from 2,000 Feet Below the Chilean Desert. 129 pp. Atheneum (Simon & Schuster Children's Publishing) 2011. ISBN 978-1-4169-1397-9 PE ISBN 978-1-4424-4025-8.

Aronson's well-researched and riveting chronicle of the Chilean mining disaster of 2010 gives readers the sense they're alongside the "thirty-three men, who had disappeared, eaten by the rock." He describes their physical hardships and emotional turmoil; he also details, in depth, the incredible topside rescue efforts. Peppered with engaging quotes, the text is fluid and attention-grabbing. Photographs and diagrams are included. Timeline, websites. Bib., glos., ind.

Central and South America; Disasters; Survival; Chile; Mines and mining

Barnard, Bryn. The Genius of Islam: How Muslims Made the Modern World. 40 pp. Knopf (Random House Children's Books) 2011. ISBN 978-0-375-84072-2 LE ISBN 978-0-375-94072-9.

This volume surveys, via text and informative original paintings, the many technological and scientific advances made, refined, or dispersed during the "Islamic Golden Age." The seventh through twelfth centuries saw progress in medicine, agriculture, optics, music, machinery, etc., to which Barnard devotes twelve topically divided double-page spreads. Tidily colored illustrations, accompanied by good captions, offer helpful amplification of the subtopics. Reading list.

Ancient and Medieval History; Islamic Empire; Religion–Islam; Inventions and inventors

Berger, Lee R. and Aronson, Marc. The Skull in the Rock: How a Scientist, a Boy, and Google Earth Opened a New Window on Human Origins. 64 pp. National (National Geographic Books) 2012. ISBN 978-1-4263-1010-2 LE ISBN 978-1-4263-1053-9.

Paleontologist Berger and son Matthew's recent find gave scientists a nearly intact skeleton from a new species, *Australopithecus sediba*. Detailed accounts of advances in the field and the supporting technology are intertwined with the story of Berger's not-always-straightforward career path. The book is enhanced by illustrative material, including photographs and striking facial reconstructions of these ancient ancestors. Reading list, websites. Glos., ind.

Prehistoric Life; Paleontology; Archaeology; Evolution; South Africa; Fossils; Anthropology

Blumenthal, Karen. Mr. Sam: How Sam Walton Built Wal-Mart and Became America's Richest Man. 186 pp. Viking 2011. ISBN 978-0-670-01177-3.

This absorbing, accessible biography chronicles the childhood, adolescence, college years, and career of Wal-Mart founder Sam Walton. Positives and negatives are explored, including Walton's personal shortcomings as well as criticisms of his company. Blumenthal has done a splendid job of not only introducing the man but also making his story relevant and timely. Vignettes, sidebars, graphs, and black-and-white photographs are included. Bib., ind.

Individual Biographies; Business; Stores; Walton, Sam

Bristow, David L. Sky Sailors: True Stories of the Balloon Era. 136 pp. Farrar 2010. ISBN 978-0-374-37014-5.

The skies were explored by various balloonists from the first flight in 1783 until the advent of the airplane. Bristow has collected nine stories about the balloon era, written in an anecdotal fashion with lots of dialogue and an emphasis on the strange, the dangerous, and the exciting. Captioned illustrations, in both color and black and white, complement the text. Bib.

Machines and Technology; Hot-air balloons; Sports–Ballooning; Flight

Brown, Don. A Wizard from the Start: The Incredible Boyhood and Amazing Inventions of Thomas Edison. 32 pp. Houghton (Houghton Mifflin Trade and Reference Division) 2010. ISBN 978-0-547-19487-5.

Young Thomas Edison worked hard, mixed chemicals, cultivated curiosity, and read a lot of books. These are the seeds of the inventor's success as presented by Brown in this unfussy picture book biography, illustrated with softly glowing watercolors. Readers will appreciate Brown's depiction of an "incredible boyhood," which here means finding one's passions at a young age and pursuing them with gusto. Bib.

Individual Biographies; Edison, Thomas A.; Inventions and inventors

Chaikin, Andrew. Mission Control, This Is Apollo: The Story of the First Voyages to the Moon. 114 pp. Viking 2009. ISBN 978-0-670-01156-8. Illustrated by Alan Bean.

With Victoria Kohl. Chaikin, drawing on his adult book *A Man on the Moon*, explores the piloted *Apollo* missions. Each of the twelve missions is covered in a detail-filled chapter, carefully outlining objectives and providing thrilling play-by-plays. The chapters flow seamlessly, allowing readers to see the missions' progression. In addition to historical photographs and technical diagrams, *Apollo*-astronaut-turned-artist Bean lends his accomplished paintings. Reading list, websites. Ind.

Space; Apollo missions; Space–Astronautics; Astronomy–Moon; Space–Space flight

Deem, James M. Bodies from the Ice: Melting Glaciers and the Recovery of the Past. 64 pp. Houghton (Houghton Mifflin Trade and Reference Division) 2008. ISBN 978-0-618-80045-2.

Deem continues his interest in mummified bodies (*Bodies from the Bog, Bodies from the Ash*) in this book that sits at the intersection of several disciplines. After introducing the oldest ice mummy (5,300-year-old Otzi), Deem gives readers a tour of mummified bodies found in ice the world over. The design, with its variety of photographs, captions, and sidebars, seals the appeal. Bib., ind.
Ancient and Medieval History; Glaciers; Mummies; Anthropology; Archaeology

 Fleming, Candace. Amelia Lost: The Life and Disappearance of Amelia Earhart. 118 pp. Random/Schwartz & Wade 2011. ISBN 978-0-375-84198-9 LE ISBN 978-0-375-94598-4.

Fleming begins her gripping narrative aboard the *Itasca*, a ship helping guide Earhart to Howland Island for refueling. The text then backs up to explore Amelia's life. Interspersed with the main text are short chapters about civilians claiming to have picked up mayday calls. The book's structure and scope, along with the story's inherent drama, provide a taut backdrop for Earhart's history. Websites. Bib., ind.
Individual Biographies; Earhart, Amelia; Women–Biographies; Women–Pilots; Pilots; Flight; Vehicles–Airplanes

Floca, Brian. Moonshot: The Flight of Apollo 11. 48 pp. Atheneum/Jackson (Simon & Schuster Children's Publishing) 2009. ISBN 978-1-4169-5046-2.

In this visually sublime, thoroughly researched picture book, Floca selects details to transform science into relatable experience. Throughout, Floca engages readers with his spare lyricism and with the artistry of his watercolor and ink pictures. He uses the format to perfection, with large pictures to communicate size, power, and perspective; sequenced panels to show steps unfolding; and small pictures to catch particular moments. Timeline.
Space; Apollo 11; Space–Space flight; Astronomy–Moon; Space–Astronautics

 Haas, Robert B. I Dreamed of Flying like a Bird: My Adventures Photographing Wild Animals from a Helicopter. 64 pp. National (National Geographic Books) 2010. ISBN 978-1-4263-0693-8 LE ISBN 978-1-4263-0694-5.

In an accessible, straightforward narrative, National Geographic aerial photographer Haas describes the unique perspective on nature to which his job makes him privy. The text fluidly combines information on animal behavior with an account of

the steps Haas takes to document it. As the exhilarating sampling of his photographs collected here demonstrates, the risks have paid off. Glos., ind.
Machines and Technology; Vehicles–Helicopters; Photography; Flight; Animals

Hodgman, Ann. The House of a Million Pets. 263 pp. Holt 2007. ISBN 978-0-8050-7974-6. Illustrated by Eugene Yelchin. Hodgman's home is a veritable ark, and that's the way she likes it. In this chatty pet-care guide meets tell-all, Hodgman dishes oodles of details about the different animals she's cared for—from guinea pigs and finches to pygmy mice and sugar gliders. Yelchin's black-and-white illustrations capture Hodgman's deep affection for her brood. Animal lovers will lap it all up.
Domestic Animals; Dwellings; Connecticut; Pets

Jurmain, Suzanne. The Secret of the Yellow Death: A True Story of Medical Sleuthing. 104 pp. Houghton (Houghton Mifflin Trade and Reference Division) 2009. ISBN 978-0-618-96581-6 PE ISBN 978-0-547-74624-1.
In this dramatic medical history, Jurmain documents the efforts of researchers in 1900 Cuba to prove or disprove the "mosquito theory" of yellow fever's transmission—by contracting the disease themselves. Above all, it's a thrilling account of the scientific process in action and of how conducting good science can involve personal risk. The succinct chapters are generously illustrated with period photos. Reading list. Bib., glos., ind.
Medicine/Human Body/and Diseases; Diseases–Yellow fever; Cuba; Scientists; Animals–Mosquitoes

Macaulay, David. Built to Last. 272 pp. Houghton (Houghton Mifflin Trade and Reference Division) 2010. ISBN 978-1-547-34240-5.
Cathedral, Castle, and *Mosque* are substantially revised for an omnibus celebration. Color has been added, and larger, more active figures heighten detail. Compositions are more animated, showing varied visual points of view. Reorganization of the texts, too, facilitates understanding of both construction processes and how the societies functioned. The whole conveys a clearer—and more dramatic—sense of the magnitude of these undertakings. Glos.
Visual Arts; Architecture; Buildings

Macaulay, David. Castle: How It Works. 32 pp. Square Fish/David Macaulay Studio 2012. ISBN 978-1-59643-744-9 PE ISBN 978-1-59643-766-1. My Readers series. With Sheila Keenan.

J
940.1

Macaulay brings his signature brand of illustrated expository nonfiction to a younger audience. This book revisits a subject Macaulay has written about previously, but presented here with the needs of developing readers in mind. Abounding with Macaulay's sly, mischievous wit, the narrative invites readers to envision themselves in the action; words and pictures work in tandem to effectively weave information into this framework. Reading list, websites. Glos., ind.
Ancient and Medieval History; Castles; War

Macaulay, David. Jet Plane: How It Works. 32 pp. Square Fish/David Macaulay Studio 2012. ISBN 978-1-59643-764-7 PE ISBN 978-1-59643-767-8. My Readers series. With Sheila Keenan.

J
629.133

Macaulay brings his signature brand of illustrated expository nonfiction to a younger audience. This book revisits a subject Macaulay has written about previously, but the topics are here presented with the needs of developing readers in mind. Notable for the amount of technical details packed into thirty-two pages, the narrative invites readers to envision themselves in the action; words and pictures effectively weave information into this framework. Reading list, websites. Glos., ind.
Machines and Technology; Vehicles–Airplanes; Flight

Matthews, Elizabeth. Different Like Coco. 40 pp. Candlewick 2007. ISBN 978-0-7636-2548-1.

Matthews presents the fashion icon Coco Chanel as a spirited girl who overcame poverty with her creativity and a lot of attitude. Chanel's confidence and originality are translated directly into her designs; the amusing pen-and-ink drawings capture her bearing and style. These selected highlights from Chanel's life present her against a backdrop of social change, celebrating her daring and independence. Timeline. Bib.
Individual Biographies; Women–Business; Women–Entrepreneurs; Women–Fashion industry;Fashion; France; Chanel, Coco; Women–Biographies; Entrepreneurship; Business; Clothing

Mitchell, Don. Driven: A Photobiography of Henry Ford. 40 pp. National (National Geographic Books) 2010. ISBN 978-1-4263-0155-1 LE ISBN 978-1-4263-0156-8.

Mitchell's brief, engaging text appraises its subject, placing him in the context of his times. Ford's contradictions make him even more fascinating; e.g., he hired disabled and minority workers but was fiercely anti-Semitic. Although this type of complexity begs for an extended treatment, Mitchell's succinct introduction successfully whets readers' appetites. The book's inviting design features an array of photographs, captions, and quotes. Reading list, timeline, websites. Ind.

Individual Biographies; Ford, Henry; Vehicles–Automobiles; Industry

Montgomery, Sy. Temple Grandin: How the Girl Who Loved Cows Embraced Autism and Changed the World. 148 pp. Houghton (Houghton Mifflin Trade and Reference Division) 2012. ISBN 978-1-547-44315-7.

Featuring a foreword by world-renowned animal-science expert Grandin, photos from her childhood and adult life, reproductions of her schematic designs for livestock facilities, and inserts on topics ranging from autism to factory farming, Montgomery's biography is full of inspiration and information. This powerful story of one amazing woman's life journey will likely help readers better understand animals and autistic people. Bib., ind.

Individual Biographies; Animal rights; Animals–Cattle; Scientists; Women–Scientists; Disabilities, Mental–Autism; Women–Biographies; Grandin, Temple

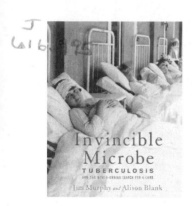

Murphy, Jim and Blank, Alison. Invincible Microbe: Tuberculosis and the Never-Ending Search for a Cure. 149 pp. Clarion 2012. ISBN 978-0-618-53574-3.

Tuberculosis has been a medical scourge through much of human history, and new drug-resistant strains keep the threat of a pandemic on the horizon. This book brings young readers up to speed with a scientific explanation of the microbe as well as medical and social histories of the disease. Despite disparate elements, the information comes together cohesively for an engaging read. Illustrations and photographs are included. Bib., ind.

Medicine/Human Body/and Diseases; Diseases–Tuberculosis; Microbiology; Epidemics

Patent, Dorothy Hinshaw. Dogs on Duty: Soldiers' Best Friends on the Battlefield and Beyond. 48 pp. Walker 2012. ISBN 978-0-8027-2845-6 LE ISBN 978-0-8027-2846-3.

Military Working Dogs have done everything from aiding the wounded during

WWI to sniffing out explosives in Iraq and Afghanistan and helping humans cope with posttraumatic stress disorder. Patent's accessible text traces the history of dogs in American wars and then outlines how a puppy becomes an MWD. "Hero Hounds" sidebars tell of individual heroic dogs. Reading list, websites. Glos., ind.

Domestic Animals; Posttraumatic stress disorder; Armed forces; Animals–Dogs; War;Soldiers

Pollan, Michael. The Omnivore's Dilemma: The Secrets Behind What You Eat. 344 pp. Dial 2009. ISBN 978-0-8037-3415-9 PE ISBN 978-0-8037-3500-2. Adapted by Richie Chevat.

This accessible adaptation of Pollan's adult bestseller *The Omnivore's Dilemma: A Natural History of Four Meals* provides abridged and/or simplified data. The book uses a recipe of science, history, and humor to create an edifying story; readers may find some of the details and photos to be disturbing. Helpful sidebars and a resources list are included. Ind.

Cookery and Nutrition; Food; Ethics

Robbins, Ken. Food for Thought: The Stories Behind the Things We Eat. 48 pp. Roaring Brook/Flash Point/Porter 2009. ISBN 978-1-59643-343-4.

Sampling significant tales, social history, and factual oddments, Robbins implicitly suggests how much there is to know about nine foods we likely take for granted. The kind of information differs from topic to topic, which may limit reference use, but readers drawn by Robbins's attractive photographic portraits of these fruits and vegetables will get an intriguing taste of wide-ranging facts and lore.

Cookery and Nutrition; Food; Folklore

Rumford, James. From the Good Mountain: How Gutenberg Changed the World. 40 pp. Roaring Brook/Flash Point/Porter 2012. ISBN 978-1-59643-542-1.

In this inviting very-first look at Gutenberg's transformative invention and the intricate craft of early printing, Rumford vivifies the ways and means of medieval innovation with intriguing details, focusing on highlights. An epilogue elucidates and extends the occasionally too-truncated information, as does handsome watercolor and gouache art that recalls illuminated manuscripts while revealing additional tasks, hazards, and sources of inspiration.

Machines and Technology; Gutenberg, Johann; Printing; Books and reading; Germany

Rusch, Elizabeth. The Mighty Mars Rovers: The Incredible Adventures of Spirit and Opportunity. 80 pp. Houghton (Houghton Mifflin Trade and Reference Division) 2012. ISBN 978-0-547-47881-4. Scientists in the Field series.

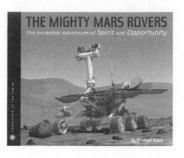

The groundbreaking 2004 Mars Exploration Rover Mission of "little" rovers *Spirit* and *Opportunity* provided evidence for the possibility of water on Mars. Principal scientist Steve Squyres's reflections frame Rusch's account, which skillfully captures the exciting quest for knowledge. Compelling images of Mars, Squyres's team, and landscapes superimposed with photos of rovers also convey this engineering accomplishment's significance. Websites. Bib., glos., ind.
Space; Scientists; Space–Space vehicles; Astronomy–Mars; Engineering; Exploration and explorers

Scott, Elaine. Buried Alive!: How 33 Miners Survived 69 Days Deep Under the Chilean Desert. 80 pp. Clarion 2012. ISBN 978-0-547-70778-5.

Using quotes liberally, Scott chronicles the 2010 San José Mine accident, favoring the human drama over the more technical aspects of the story. The book has a large trim size and numerous full-color photographs of the mine site, the families who waited there for weeks, the equipment used to rescue the miners, and ultimately the miners themselves. Bib., glos., ind.
Central and South America; Accidents; Mines and mining; Chile; Rescue work; Disasters; Survival

Scott, Elaine. Space, Stars, and the Beginning of Time: What the Hubble Telescope Saw. 66 pp. Clarion 2011. ISBN 978-0-547-24189-0.

Scott covers the last approved repair mission for the Hubble Telescope (in 2009) as well as highlights of the Hubble-supported science and technology advancements of the past two decades. While the book is filled with amazingly clear, color-enhanced images of planets, stars, etc., Scott also explains the less showy but significant science made possible by the Hubble's instruments. Reading list, websites. Glos., ind.
Space; Hubble Space Telescope

Sobol, Richard. The Story of Silk: From Worm Spit to Woven Scarves. 40 pp. Candlewick 2012. ISBN 978-0-7636-4165-8. Traveling Photographer series.

From the arrival of tiny eggs to the growth of silkworms in baskets of mulberry leaves, the cooking of cocoons, and the creation of cloth, Sobol describes the stages of creating silk in lively writing and abundant photographs. With an apprecia-

tion for these Thai villagers and their culture, Sobol makes their story come alive in this follow-up to *The Life of Rice*. Glos.
Farm Life/Husbandry/and Gardening; Silk; Thailand

Walker, Sally M. Written in Bone: Buried Lives of Jamestown and Colonial Maryland. 144 pp. Carolrhoda 2009. ISBN 978-0-8225-7135-3.

With precise detail and meticulous description, Walker follows a forensic anthropologist and his team of scientists, historians, and archaeologists as they uncover human remains and other artifacts. Their excavations take them through a cross-section of people, from wealthy colonial leaders to indentured servants and African slaves. The book design is unified in its thoughtful use of layout, color, illustrations, and fonts. Timeline. Bib., ind.
North America; Forensic science; Paleontology; Archaeology; Anthropology; History, American–Colonial life; Jamestown (VA); Maryland; Fossils

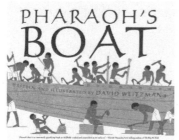

Weitzman, David. Pharaoh's Boat. 48 pp. Houghton (Houghton Mifflin Trade and Reference Division) 2009. ISBN 978-0-547-05341-7.

This handsome casebook on constructing (and, more than four thousand years later, *re*constructing) the boat Pharaoh Cheops would ride into the afterlife focuses on intricacies of design and creation. Clear schematic drawings of the boat's parts and assemblage are effectively, dramatically set against plenty of white space. A valedictory double-gatefold spread shows the reconstructed vessel manned by ancient oarsmen. A map is appended.
Ancient and Medieval History; Vehicles–Boats and boating; Egypt, Ancient; Kings, queens, and rulers; Archaeology

Weitzman, David. Skywalkers: Mohawk Ironworkers Build the City. 124 pp. Roaring Brook/Flash Point 2010. ISBN 978-1-59643-162-1.

Mohawks have been in high steel for more than a hundred years, since construction of the first railroad bridge over the St. Lawrence in 1886. Throughout this useful book, Weitzman effectively mingles social and industrial history to tell the mens' story. Ironworker testimony, along with other eyewitness reports, gives the volume a documentary, you-are-there feel. Historical photographs appear throughout. Bib., glos., ind.
Native Americans; Skyscrapers; Native Americans–North America–Mohawk; City and town life; Construction; Buildings; Architecture; Work

Folklore

When Apples Grew Noses and White Horses Flew

Tales of TI-JEAN

Jan Andrews

Pictures by Dušan Petričić

Andrews, Jan. When Apples Grew Noses and White Horses Flew: Tales of Ti-Jean. 69 pp. Groundwood (House of Anansi Press) 2011. ISBN 978-0-88899-952-8. Illustrated by Dušan Petričić.

Ti-Jean, cheerful, hapless stripling of French-Canadian folklore, makes a winning appearance in three tales of European origin lightly transposed to a New World setting. Andrews is a storyteller, and these zesty, well-paced texts virtually read themselves. Source notes are appended, but these are not so much retellings or even adaptations as simpatico re-imaginings. Petričić's sly drawings underpin the fun throughout.

Folktales/Myths/and Legends; French Canadians

Berner, Rotraut Susanne. Definitely Not for Little Ones: Some Very Grimm Fairy-Tale Comics. 48 pp. Groundwood (House of Anansi Press) 2009. ISBN 978-0-88899-957-3. Translated by Shelley Tanaka.

Berner presents eight cartoon-strip versions of Grimm stories. Straightforward, pared-down translations with mild demotic touches (e.g., Rapunzel's rueful complaint, "Oh, brother, not again") are accompanied by sometimes cheeky drawings of a folktale world featuring wishing wells and wolves and hedgehogs playing bagpipes. The format works perfectly with the material; this would be a fine first Grimm for the older elementary-school crowd.

Folktales/Myths/and Legends; Books in translation; Grimm, Jacob and Wilhelm; Cartoons and comics

Bowman, James Cloyd. Pecos Bill: The Greatest Cowboy of All Time. 254 pp. NYRB (The New York Review of Books) 2007. ISBN 978-1-59017-224-7. Illustrated by Laura Bannon. Reissue, 1937, Whitman.

This Newbery Honor Book includes nineteen tall tales that detail the exploits of super-cowboy Pecos Bill in the American West. The stories were originally told at round-

ups and around campfires, and Bowman's writing exemplifies the gusto and broad humor of cowboy life. Strong-lined black-and-white drawings illustrate the tales.
Folktales/Myths/and Legends; Folklore–United States; Cowboys; Tall tales; West (U.S.); History, American–Frontier and pioneer life

○ **Calcutt, David.** Robin Hood. 176 pp. Barefoot 2012. PE ISBN 978-1-84686-799-6. Illustrated by Grahame Baker-Smith.
A playwright retells nine of the legendary hero's more familiar adventures, from Robin's first becoming an outlaw to a "last battle." Pitching to middle-grade readers, Calcutt writes in brief declarative sentences and lively dialogue lightened with a few modern colloquialisms. Baker-Smith's mixed-media, digitally blended illustrations feature craggily heroic, dramatically shadowed figures; delicate, misty landscapes and woodland creatures in occasional spot art add variety.
Folktales/Myths/and Legends; Robin Hood (Legendary character); Legends–England; Thieves

○ **Frisch, Aaron.** The Girl in Red. 32 pp. Creative Editions 2012. ISBN 978-1-56846-223-3. Illustrated by Roberto Innocenti. series. Story by Roberto Innocenti.
Little Red travels a 'hood of a different color in this gritty adaptation. The story begins in a crumbling housing project; along the way Red meets with "jackal" hooligans and a motorcycle-riding "wolf"; we last see her at the door of Nana's trailer, in which we know the wolf waits. Innocenti sets a menacing scene through his terse narrative and dark illustrations.
Folktales/Myths/and Legends; City and town life

○ **Hayes, Joe.** The Coyote Under the Table / El coyote debajo de la mesa: Folktales Told in Spanish and English. 133 pp. Cinco 2011. ISBN 978-1-935955-21-4 PE ISBN 978-1-935955-06-1. Illustrated by Antonio Castro L.
Hayes's latest collection of bilingual folktales drawn from the Hispanic New Mexico oral tradition provides refreshing depth and humor. Brief source notes expand on the history of each of the ten tales and add social/historical context. Clean, unencumbered prose draws attention to the structure and rhythm of the stories, which are best read aloud. Amusing illustrations face the start of each entry.
Folktales/Myths/and Legends; Folklore–New Mexico; Bilingual books; Foreign languages —Spanish language

McBratney, Sam. One Voice, Please: Favorite Read-Aloud Stories. 167 pp. Candlewick 2008. ISBN 978-0-7636-3479-7 PE ISBN 978-0-7445-8331-1. Illustrated by Russell Ayto.

These fifty-six short fables, cautionary tales, and anecdotes tickle mind and funny bone with unexpected twists of logic. Ayto's angular drawings punctuate the pages with their own lighthearted take on wise men, fools, and tricksters. Coming from such sources as the Bible and Aesop, many of the stories will be familiar to adults (though there are no source notes).

Folktales/Myths/and Legends; Short stories; Storytelling; Humorous stories

Mitchell, Stephen. Genies, Meanies, and Magic Rings: Three Tales from The Arabian Nights. 181 pp. Walker 2007. ISBN 978-0-8027-9639-4. Illustrated by Tom Pohrt.

In addition to "Ali Baba and the Forty Thieves" and "Aladdin and the Magic Lamp," Mitchell includes the lesser-known "Abu Keer and Abu Seer." Mitchell delights in exaggeration and embroiders these already outrageous tales with extended descriptions of jewels and riches, clothing and food, sneaking in references to chocolate chip cookies to entice modern readers. Black-and-white line illustrations round out these retellings.

Folktales/Myths/and Legends; Folklore–Arab countries

Schlitz, Laura Amy. The Bearskinner: A Tale of the Brothers Grimm. 40 pp. Candlewick 2007. ISBN 978-0-7636-2730-0. Illustrated by Max Grafe.

An ex-soldier accepts a hard bargain: he'll be rich forever if, for seven years, he wears the skin of a bear; failure means eternal perdition. Schlitz narrates with clarity and grace. Except for the devil's green coat, Grafe's atmospheric full-page illustrations are almost monochromatic, composed of grays and browns with an occasional wash of blue, gleam of gold, or sunset hue.

Folktales/Myths/and Legends; Folklore–Germany; Emotions–Love; Animals–Bears; Soldiers; Devil; Grimm, Jacob and Wilhelm

Williams, Marcia. The Elephant's Friend and Other Tales from Ancient India. 40 pp. Candlewick 2012. ISBN 978-0-7636-5916-5 PE ISBN 978-0-7636-7055-9.

Williams adapts eight fables from Indian folklore; each tale leads, satisfyingly, to its just conclusion—and to a wisdom that transcends the stories' seemingly simple events. Well-told in narrative captions, the tales are much enhanced by comically informal remarks in speech balloons. Williams's ebullient gouache illustrations are in jewel-like tones of Indian art. A grand introduction to these venerable stories.

Folktales/Myths/and Legends; Folklore–India; Folklore–Animals; Fables; Cartoons and comics

Language & Literature

Dubosarsky, Ursula. The Word Snoop. 246 pp. Dial 2009. ISBN 978-0-8037-3406-7. Illustrated by Tohby Riddle.

In the guise of the eponymous Word Snoop, Dubosarsky delivers a cursory, chatty tour of the evolution of the English language from ancient to modern times. She covers expected topics (spelling, punctuation) in addition to a potpourri of lesser-known tidbits; her enthusiasm for the intricacies and oddities of the English language is infectious. Pen-and-ink drawings help keep the lessons light. Glos.
General Language; English language

Kerley, Barbara. The Extraordinary Mark Twain (According to Susy). 48 pp. Scholastic 2010. ISBN 978-0-545-12508-6. Illustrated by Edwin Fotheringham.

Thirteen-year-old Susy Clemens's biography of her father informs this account covering both biographer and biographee. Kerley details Susy's process of writing about and observing her father, using primary sources and inserting seven small facsimiles of Susy's journal pages into the book. Fotheringham's muted palette and large, sturdy illustrations provide discreet counterpoint to a complicated design. Timeline.
Individual Biographies; Clemens, Susy; Twain, Mark; Authors; Family–Father and daughter; Writing

McDonough, Yona Zeldis. Louisa: The Life of Louisa May Alcott. 48 pp. Holt/Ottaviano 2009. ISBN 978-0-8050-8192-3. Illustrated by Bethanne Andersen.

McDonough describes the Alcotts' uncompromising ideals, Louisa's struggles with poverty, her growing fame, and her loyal nurturing of a family sadly diminished by its losses over time. The informative, no-nonsense text and the sophisticated illustrations should appeal to readers who are nearly ready for *Little Women* itself. Andersen's gouache and pastel art is rendered with a free-flowing, impressionistic brush. Timeline. Bib.

Individual Biographies; Women–Authors; Alcott, Louisa May; Women–Biographies; Authors; Children's literature

Marcus, Leonard S. Funny Business: Conversations with Writers of Comedy. 214 pp. Candlewick 2009. ISBN 978-0-7636-3254-0.

Marcus questions twelve writers, including Daniel Handler, Beverly Cleary, and Louis Sachar, about childhood, personality, working methods, reading, and approaches to comedy. The portraits are fleshed out with photos, booklists, and marked-up manuscript pages. The wisest line goes to Norton Juster: "One of the bugaboos of our lives is having always to stay in context."

General Literature; Children's literature; Authors; Humorous stories

J 411 R **Robb, Don.** Ox, House, Stick: The History of Our Alphabet. 48 pp. Charlesbridge 2007. ISBN 978-1-57091-609-0 PE ISBN 978-1-57091-610-6. Illustrated by Anne Smith.

Robb traces each letter's transformations, grouping those with intertwined histories and tucking in lots of fascinating lore. Pleasantly open spreads accommodate basic facts in a Roman face, ancillary information in sans serif, plus an abundance of illustrative details—letters in their various forms, artifacts, and details of ancient settings. An excellent first resource, skillfully organized to introduce the subject and inspire interest. Reading list, websites. Bib.

General Language; History, World; Alphabet

Rumford, James. Beowulf: A Hero's Tale Retold. 48 pp. Houghton (Houghton Mifflin Trade and Reference Division) 2007. ISBN 978-0-618-75637-7.

Rumford's version of the epic Anglo-Saxon poem is superb on all counts—from the elegant bookmaking to the vigorous, evocative, yet concise prose to the pen-and-ink and watercolor illustrations. The story's three distinct parts are delineated by green, blue, and yellow backgrounds. Most effective is the dragon lurking behind the panels of the first two sections, foreshadowing Beowulf's eventual fate.

General Literature; Dragons; Monsters; Heroes; England; Kings, queens, and rulers

Scieszka, Jon. Knucklehead: Tall Tales & Mostly True Stories About Growing Up Scieszka. 112 pp. Viking 2008. ISBN 978-0-670-01106-3 PE ISBN 978-0-670-01138-4.

Scieszka offers entertaining and allegedly true tales from his Michigan childhood, growing up in a family of six boys and two blessedly good-natured parents. Short, conversational paragraphs showcase his expertly timed delivery. The anecdotes are loosely chronological but discrete, and the book's browsability is enhanced by a profusion of family photos. There's also a helpful index: "smartest, 11; *see also* Jon."

Individual Biographies; Humorous stories; Family–Parent and child; Writing; Authors; Children's literature; Scieszka, Jon; Michigan; Family–Siblings; Autobiographies

Warren, Andrea. Charles Dickens and the Street Children of London. 156 pp. Houghton (Houghton Mifflin Trade and Reference Division) 2011. ISBN 978-0-547-39574-6. Warren focuses on how Dickens's impoverished childhood led to a deep sense of empathy that manifested itself in his writing and his life. Young Charles was largely self-educated; when he became a writer, he infused his novels with his own experiences and observations of rundown London. Warren generally sticks to her focus, but the narrative also takes some interesting diversions. Websites. Bib., ind.

Individual Biographies; London (England); Authors; Dickens, Charles; Victorian England; Poverty; Children; Homelessness

Williams, Marcia. Chaucer's Canterbury Tales. 48 pp. Candlewick 2007. ISBN 978-0-7636-3197-0.

Williams adapts nine tales, each presented in comic-strip-style panels. A chorus provides running commentary, unobtrusively allowing the author to braid Chaucer's storytelling contest into her retelling. The bright cartoons make the most of Chaucer's bawdiness, exaggerating physical faults and reveling in potty humor. The straightforward telling reflects an oral style and allows the illustrations to carry both narrative suspense and humor.

General Literature; Storytelling; England; Chaucer, Geoffrey; Middle Ages; Cartoons and comics; Humorous stories

—FOCUS ON—

Charles Dickens

Happy Birthday, Mr. Dickens!

By Jill Maza

Jill Heritage Maza is the Head of libraries at Montclair (NJ) Kimberley Academy.

As we marked the 200th anniversary of Charles Dickens's birth, there was no doubt that the celebrated author was alive and well in the hearts and minds of readers. Never, it seems, has the timelessness of his work been more apparent. In honor of his bicentennial, websites, celebrations, essay contests, exhibitions, and, of course, a rash of new books exploring the man and his work have emerged.

Born to an upper-middle-class family in 1812, he turned toward the plight of London's poor after an early experience laboring in a blacking (shoe polish) factory while his father was in debtor's prison. Though his fame reached mythic proportions within his own lifetime, Dickens never strayed from his mission to address society's ills through his literature and charitable work. It cannot be said, however, that he remained as faithful or steady in the treatment of those closest to him, including his family. It is precisely this combination of a colorful, sometimes sordid personal life and a brilliant body of work that has proven so irresistible to generations of biographers and now fiction writers and graphic novelists.

The titles that follow range from exhaustively researched biographies and the latest editions of Dickens's works to fresh graphic adaptations and fiction that seamlessly weaves in Dickensian references and literary devices. Does that copy of *A Christmas Carol* on your shelf look a little tattered? Are you in need of material for the Dickens amateur or budding Victorian scholar? Simply fancy a good read with a little Dickensian darkness mixed in for good measure? There's never been a better time to update a collection. For modern readers, young and old, seeking comedy, satire, social activism, and intrigue, Dickens continues to deliver.

BIOGRAPHIES & NONFICTION

 Manning, Mick & Brita Granström. Charles Dickens: Scenes from an Extraordinary Life. illus. by authors. Frances Lincoln. 2011. Tr $18.95. ISBN 978-1-84780-187-6.

Gr 4-7–The authors chronologically construct this picture-book-length portrait around quotes from Dickens's books and letters. A snippet from *David Copperfield* that alludes to Dickens's birth, for example, launches the first spread. A fresh approach that incorporates graphic-novel-style illustrative elements and breaks the biography into manageable pieces for novices.

 **Osborne, Mary Pope & Natalie Pope Boyce.** Rags and Riches: Kids in the Time of Charles Dickens. Bk. 22. illus. by Sal Murdocca. (Magic Tree House Research Guide Series). Random. 2010. PLB $12.99. ISBN 978-0-375-96010-9; pap. $4.99. ISBN 978-0-375-86010-2.

Gr 3-6–A companion to *A Ghost Tale for Christmas Time* (Random, 2010), this guide answers Jack and Annie's (and presumably readers') questions about what everyday life was like for children in Victorian England. A blend of text and illustrations succinctly, yet colorfully, depicts the child's world of 19th-century England, presenting difficult issues in easy-to-understand language.

Rosen, Michael. Dickens: His Work and His World. illus. by Robert Ingpen. Candlewick. 2005. RTE $19.99. ISBN 978-0-763-62752-2; pap. $10.99. ISBN 978-0-763-63888-7.

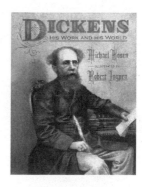

Gr 5-8–An excellent introduction to Dickens for neophytes, this title explores Dickens's life and 19th-century London before diving into a basic literary study of four of his best-known works: *A Christmas Carol*, *Oliver Twist*, *David Copperfield*, and *Great Expectations*. Ingpen's rich watercolors punctuate and dramatize the text.

Warren, Andrea. Charles Dickens and the Street Children of London. Houghton Harcourt. 2011. Tr $18.99. ISBN 978-0-547-39574-6.

Gr 5-8–The zealousness with which Dickens championed London's poor serves as the basis for this thought-provoking, well-researched, and accessible title. Warren expertly weaves Dickens's biography into the plight of Victorian London's poorest children and explores the evolution of child labor through contemporary times. Evocative photographs and reproductions give a face to the faceless and to the writer's life.

Wells-Cole, Catherine. Charles Dickens: England's Most Captivating Storyteller. (Historical Notebooks Series). Candlewick/Templar. 2011. Tr $19.99. ISBN 978-0-7636-5567-9.

Gr 3-6–A scrapbook homage, this title's gorgeous, high-quality reproductions make a strong visual impact. Flaps, folds, and envelopes hiding letters, maps, and excerpts make readers work to uncover information in the author's "notebook." Children will be quickly drawn into the hunt for more treasured tidbits about Dickens, his work, and Victorian England.

FICTION

Buzbee, Lewis. The Haunting of Charles Dickens. illus. by Greg Ruth. Feiwel & Friends. 2009. Tr $17.99. ISBN 978-0-312-38256-8; ebook $9.99. ISBN 978-1-4299-6174-5.

Gr 5-8–Meg's older brother, Orion, has mysteriously disappeared. Unable to bear his absence, the 12-year-old steals away one evening and sights him in an unlikely place. That same night, she bumps into her family print shop's famous patron, Charles Dickens, and the pair partner to bring Orion home. Naturalistic black-and-white drawings bring the tale to life.

Deedy, Carmen Agra & Randall Wright. The Cheshire Cheese Cat: A Dickens of a Tale. illus. by Barry Moser. Peachtree. 2011. Tr $16.95. ISBN 978-1-56145-595-9.

Gr 5-8–Alley cat Skilley finagles his way off the tough streets of London and into a life as a mouser at a local inn where he strikes up an unlikely alliance with the resident mouse and befriends Dickens. A zany scheme and high jinks ensue. Dickensian references pepper this playful, clever tale illustrated with pencil drawings.

Hopkinson, Deborah. A Boy Called Dickens. illus. by John Hendrix. Random/Schwartz & Wade Bks. Jan. 2012. Tr $17.99. ISBN 978-0-375-86732-3; PLB $20.99. ISBN 978-0-375-96732-0.

Gr 3-6–Hopkinson captures a snapshot of time in young Dickens's life, from a day spent spinning tales in the factory to his long-awaited reinstatement in school. A final nod is given to his ultimate success as a writer and the role played by characters from his boyhood. Spectacular, full-bleed, mixed-media illustrations bring the book to another level.

Osborne, Mary Pope. A Ghost Tale for Christmas Time. Bk. 44. illus. by Sal Murdocca. (Magic Tree House Series/A Merlin Mission). Random. 2010. Tr $15.99. ISBN 978-0-375-85652-5; PLB $18.99. ISBN 978-0-375-95652-2; ebook $9.99. ISBN 978-0-375-89467-1.

Gr 2-4–Jack and Annie travel to Victorian England and meet Dickens, who is suffering from writer's block (as he was famously known to do). The siblings take a page right out of Dickens's own book and summon the ghosts of Christmas past, present, and future, an act they hope will result in the publication of *A Christmas Carol*.

GRAPHIC NOVELS

Dickens, Charles. Great Expectations. Bk. 1. adapt. and illus. by Rick Geary. (Classics Illustrated). Papercutz. 2008. Tr $9.95. ISBN 978-1-59707-097-3.

Gr 5-8–A few years ago, this edition launched the new generation of Classics Illustrated titles. Though this graphic adaptation is succinct, it captures the spirit of the original tale through lively text and Geary's signature comically flat style. A worthy introduction to readers on the verge of readiness for the actual text.

Dickens, Charles. Great Expectations: The Graphic Novel: Original Text. ISBN 978-1-906332-59-4.

——.Great Expectations: The Graphic Novel: Quick Text. ISBN 978-1-906332-60-0.

ea vol: adapt. by Jen Green. illus. by John Stokes, et al. Classical Comics. 2009. pap. $16.95.

Gr 5-8–Available in two versions, these graphic adaptations were crafted for instructional purposes and are designed to provide two very different access points. While it could be debated that the text, especially in the "quick" version, is too stripped down, the incorporated teacher resources and the opportunity for differentiation will be worth the purchase for many educators.

A CHRISTMAS CAROL/RECENT ILLUSTRATED EDITIONS

Dickens, Charles. A Christmas Carol. adapt. by Josh Greenhut. illus. by Brett Helquist. HarperCollins. 2009. Tr $17.99. ISBN 978-0-06-165099-4; PLB $18.89. ISBN 978-0-06-165100-7.

Gr 3-6–Who better than the illustrator of Lemony Snicket's Dickensian "A Series of Unfortunate Events" to present the master's timeless tale in a picture book? Helquist's composition draws readers' eyes to Scrooge on every page, often crafting the mood of the tale through the expressions on Ebenezer's oversize features. An abridged text renders the tale accessible to a younger audience.

Dickens, Charles. A Christmas Carol. adapt. by Stephen Krensky. illus. by Dean Morrissey. HarperCollins. 2004. pap. $7.99. ISBN 978-0-06-443606-9.

Gr 4-7–The realism of Morrissey's rich illustrations dramatically heightens the tale's immediacy in this successful adaptation. Interior scenes, evocative of Dutch oil paintings in their purposeful use of light and dark, pull readers into intimate moments throughout the book. An excellent option for those ready to move beyond picture-book adaptations.

J Fic

Dickens, Charles. A Christmas Carol. illus. by P.J. Lynch. Candlewick. 2006. RTE $19.99. ISBN 978-0-763-63120-8.

Gr 5-8–Lynch's dark and brooding, ethereal illustrations are pitch-perfect in this beautifully imagined version of the tale. The artist moves from full spreads of breathtaking landscapes to framed views of quiet interior scenes with ease, echoing the pace of the tale as Scrooge is whisked from place to place across time and then pulled into quiet, intimate moments.

ON THE WEB

The Cheshire Cheese Cat. cheshirecheesecat.com. Peachtree. (Accessed 11/23/11).

Gr 5-8–Whether or not viewers have read Carmen Agra Deedy and Randall Wright's *The Cheshire Cheese Cat* (Peachtree, 2011), there is much to be found on this companion site about Dickens, Victorian London, and the Tower of London. A "Resources" section provides classroom activities for each of the topics as well as a printable "Teacher's Guide" to the book.

Eds. Note: The full version of the "Happy Birthday,
Mr. Dickens," is available online at http://bit.ly/19M2iGu

Poetry

Brooks, Gwendolyn. Bronzeville Boys and Girls. 48 pp. HarperCollins/Amistad 2007. ISBN 978-0-06-029505-9 LE ISBN 978-0-06-029506-6. Illustrated by Faith Ringgold. New ed., 1956.

With acute observation and feeling, Brooks captures moments of childhood. Ringgold wisely sets her pictures in the time (1956) and place (the Bronzeville neighborhood of Chicago) of the original writing. The strong colors help situate the poems both in the real world and the imaginary world of childhood, where a tea party seems to float in the air on a raft of blue.

Poetry; African Americans; Chicago (IL); City and town life

Florian, Douglas. Comets, Stars, the Moon, and Mars: Space Poems and Paintings. 48 pp. Harcourt (Harcourt Trade Publishers) 2007. ISBN 978-0-15-205372-7.

Moving from universe to galaxy to sun, planets to constellations and "the great beyond," Florian sums up the heavens in twenty snappy rhymes. Variants of flame-orange and blues predominate in the full-spread paintings, which incorporate collage-like accents. With its gorgeous palette, sweeping vistas, and ingenious effects (including occasional die-cut holes), this is an expansive and illuminating view of the subject. Bib., glos.

Poetry; Humorous poetry; Astronomy; Space

Florian, Douglas. Dinothesaurus. 48 pp. Atheneum (Simon & Schuster Children's Publishing) 2009. ISBN 978-1-4169-7978-4.

Beginning by defining "The Age of Dinosaurs" and ending with the creatures' demise, Florian rounds up the usual prehistoric suspects and adds a few lesser knowns (*Minmi, Troodon*). The twenty resultant verses are characterized by clever wordplay, sophisticated mixed-media illustrations, and a scientific fact or two, emphasizing Florian's genius for fusing accessible language, image, and science. Dinosaur museums and fossil sites are listed. Reading list.

Poetry; Prehistoric life–Dinosaurs; Humorous poetry

George, Kristine O'Connell. Emma Dilemma: Big Sister Poems. 48 pp. Clarion 2011. ISBN 978-0-618-42842-7. Illustrated by Nancy Carpenter.

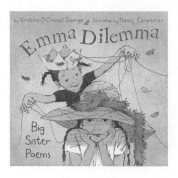

Thirty-four poems cover the highs and lows of big sisterhood. Fourth-grader Jess describes life with almost-four-year-old Emma, who adores and simultaneously annoys her sister. The straightforward, honest poems contain a range of feelings: embarrassment, fury, affection. Likewise, Carpenter's illustrations capture both the endearing and irritating qualities of preschool-aged girls, while the expressions on Jess's face capture every nuance of her emotions. *Poetry; Family–Siblings*

Hughes, Ted. Collected Poems for Children. 259 pp. Farrar 2007. ISBN 978-0-374-31429-3 PE ISBN 978-0-374-41309-5. Illustrated by Raymond Briggs.
The book begins with a seal birthing awake into the sea and ends with a lamb dying into the chaotic abyss. In between there is wonder. Every page reveals a glimpse of life at once familiar and utterly strange. Briggs's soft black-and-white charcoal sketches are, mainly, doodles in the margins; the best ones amplify something implicit in the poems. *Poetry*

Issa, Kobayashi. Today and Today. 40 pp. Scholastic 2007. ISBN 978-0-439-59078-5. Illustrated by G. Brian Karas.
Eighteen haiku by the famous poet are illustrated with pictures that tell about one year in the life of a contemporary family. Karas's art captures moments in time and conveys, with color and light, sensory detail. This contemplative and lushly illustrated book adds a new dimension to the usual study of the haiku form. *Poetry; Poetry–Haiku; Seasons; Family*

Janeczko, Paul B. A Foot in the Mouth: Poems to Speak, Sing, and Shout. 64 pp. Candlewick 2009. ISBN 978-0-7636-0663-3 PE ISBN 978-0-7636-6083-3. Illustrated by Chris Raschka.
These thirty-eight works celebrate the aurality of poetry. Some of the organization is by number of readers (poems to read alone, in two voices, etc.), others highlight form (limericks, list poems), while another section includes bilingual poems in Spanish and English. Raschka's boldly outlined, impressionistic illustra-

tions emphasize speaker or subject through whimsical combinations of watercolors and torn paper. A collection to savor.

Poetry Collections

Janeczko, Paul B. Hey, You!: Poems to Skyscrapers, Mosquitoes, and Other Fun Things. 40 pp. HarperCollins 2007. ISBN 978-0-06-052347-3 LE ISBN 978-0-06-052348-0. Illustrated by Robert Rayevsky.

This collection includes a few classic poems; most of the works, though, are new and fresh. They range widely in tone from the frivolous to the heartfelt, and the book flows beautifully from subject to subject. Rayevsky's brush-inked and watercolor illustrations add visual appeal and gentle humor without overwhelming the words. Surprising and inspiring.

Poetry Collections; Humorous poetry

Lewis, J. Patrick. The World's Greatest: Poems. 32 pp. Chronicle 2008. ISBN 978-0-8118-5130-5. Illustrated by Keith Graves.

Each of the twenty-five works in this inventive collection is based on a *Guinness Book of World Records* entry. Some are not unexpected while others are more bizarre ("The Most Cobras Kissed Consecutively"). Lewis varies his style to best accommodate the feat described. Likewise, Graves's acrylic and colored-pencil illustrations take different forms and as much space as they need to illuminate the poems.

Poetry; Humorous poetry

Nye, Naomi Shihab. Honeybee. 164 pp. Greenwillow (HarperCollins Children's Books Group) 2008. ISBN 978-0-06-085390-7 LE ISBN 978-0-06-085391-4.

These eighty-two poems and prose paragraphs cover prejudice, kindness, war, and peace. Nye's introduction discusses America's "busy bee" climate and the importance of "dipping and diving down into the nectar of scenes" and sweet moments. In some pieces, bee-related words and facts buzz in and out, and readers will sense the connections (and disconnections) between humans and honeybees.

Poetry; Animals–Bees

Park, Linda Sue. Tap Dancing on the Roof: Sijo (Poems). 40 pp. Clarion 2007. ISBN 978-0-618-23483-7. Illustrated by Istvan Banyai.

Park presents twenty-seven *sijo* (traditional humorous and/or ironic three-line Korean poetry) about seasons, home, and school. Her poems go beyond culture and personal sensibility and strike at common human experience. Banyai's illustrations enhance the collection with an extra element of wit and imaginative freedom; he staves off sentiment with retro-style cartoons, carefree lines, and playful interpretations of the verbal text.
Poetry; Poetry–Sijo

Prelutsky, Jack. The Swamps of Sleethe: Poems from Beyond the Solar System. 40 pp. Knopf (Random House Children's Books) 2009. ISBN 978-0-375-84674-8 LE ISBN 978-0-375-94674-5. Illustrated by Jimmy Pickering.

Prelutsky takes readers to planets they've never heard of—and wouldn't want to visit (e.g., Swole, where you can't stop crying; Skreber, where you can't stop laughing). This macabre journey isn't for the faint of heart or lazy of mind; Prelutsky's meter rewards careful ears while trusting readers to figure out words like "cataclysmic" and "unconscionably." Pickering's comically creepy illustrations enhance the strangeness.
Poetry; Extraterrestrial beings; Humorous poetry; Space

Raczka, Bob. Lemonade, and Other Poems Squeezed from a Single Word. 44 pp. Roaring Brook 2011. ISBN 978-1-59643-541-4 PE ISBN 978-1-250-01894-6. Illustrated by Nancy Doniger.

In this volume, poet meets Scrabble nerd. Raczka makes poems from a single word by rearranging various letters from that word, anagram-style. Some are imagistic: "moonlight" is "hot / night / thin / light / moth / in / motion." Some are mini-narratives: "friend" is "fred / finds / ed." The concrete poem format makes you want to try some yourself.
Poetry; Language–Anagrams; Poetry–Concrete poems

Walker, Alice. Why War Is Never a Good Idea. 32 pp. HarperCollins 2007. ISBN 978-0-06-075385-6 LE ISBN 978-0-06-075386-3. Illustrated by Stefano Vitale.

Walker's ceaseless rhythm echoes the inexorable march of war. Poignancy is sustained in gentle images until war flaunts its power. With a creative economy of words, Walker offers a challenge: Will war continue as humanity's legacy? From

Vitale's palette come illustrations that show, through color and light, the striking contrast between peace and safety and the devastation of war.

Poetry; War; Violence; Peace

Wong, Janet S. Twist: Yoga Poems. 40 pp. McElderry (Simon & Schuster Children's Publishing) 2007. ISBN 978-0-689-87394-2. Illustrated by Julie Paschkis.

Most of the sixteen poems in this book focus on a particular yoga pose. Wong's verses effectively evoke their subjects, and Paschkis's elegant watercolors swirl with movement. Framed illustrations depict each pose, while animals, people, and related objects border the frame with Indian motifs. Suitable both for readers already familiar with yoga and those just getting started.

Poetry; Sports–Yoga

Worth, Valerie. Animal Poems. 48 pp. Farrar 2007. ISBN 978-0-374-38057-1. Illustrated by Steve Jenkins.

This posthumous collection features twenty-three animal poems in free verse. Worth uses common language uncommonly, rich with sound sameness and repetition. Master cut-paper artist Jenkins matches the verbal surprises with his own visual revelations. Without background clutter, each double-page spread devotes itself to a single poem and image, impressive and regal in their cumulative effect.

Poetry; Animals

Religion & Myth

Curlee, Lynn. Mythological Creatures: A Classical Bestiary. 40 pp. Atheneum (Simon & Schuster Children's Publishing) 2008. ISBN 978-1-4169-1453-2.

This book provides an eye-catching introduction to sixteen mythological creatures of ancient Greece. Straightforward and clean, the text outlines without dramatization what the mythical beings were and describes their roles in Greek lore. Confining each within a broad, sober border, Curlee depicts all as classically statuesque; even such horrors as Cyclops, blood streaming down his arms, seem congealed in the moment.

Folktales/Myths/and Legends; Folklore–Animals; Mythology, Greek

Demi. The Legend of Lao Tzu and the Tao Te Ching. 48 pp. McElderry (Simon & Schuster Children's Publishing) 2007. ISBN 978-1-4169-1206-4.

Demi presents the legendary figure "who may or may not have been born; who may or may not have founded Taoism." Elegant, minimally limned figures and gold-colored text, all set on circles of lightly clouded blue sky, make a sumptuous package. Twenty verses from the *Tao Te Ching* are included. Many Taoist symbols (including the familiar yin/yang) are shown and defined.

General Religion; Religion–Taoism; China, Ancient; Lao Tzu; Legends–China

Lunge-Larsen, Lise. Gifts from the Gods: Ancient Words and Wisdom from Greek and Roman Mythology. 96 pp. Houghton (Houghton Mifflin Trade and Reference Division) 2011. ISBN 978-0-547-15229-5. Illustrated by Gareth Hinds.

From "Achilles' heel" to "victory," Lunge-Larsen explores how words have been derived from myths. Each entry begins with a definition plus a quote that incorporates it. Next comes the relevant myth, along with graphic-novel–style art, its pencil and watercolor renditions enlivening the straightforward text with eloquent gestures and expressions. The classic tales and lively pictures make an effective lure to etymology's dramatic possibilities. Bib., ind.

Folktales/Myths/and Legends; Gods and goddesses; Mythology, Roman; Mythology, Greek; Language–Vocabulary

Lupton, Hugh and Morden, Daniel. The Adventures of Achilles. 128 pp. Barefoot 2012. PE ISBN 978-1-84686-800-9. Illustrated by Carole Hénaff.

Two practiced British storytellers focus on the titular warrior for a succinct account of the Trojan War, supplementing Homer's *Iliad* with other ancient sources (an author's note would have helped). Expertly honed language moves the events along swiftly. Acrylic illustrations, bright with Attic red and Aegean blue, recall ancient Greek art and second the meaning of the text without competing with it.

Folktales/Myths/and Legends; Trojan War; Gods and goddesses; War; Mythology, Greek; Greece, Ancient

Napoli, Donna Jo. Treasury of Greek Mythology: Classic Stories of Gods, Goddesses, Heroes & Monsters. 192 pp. National (National Geographic Books) 2011. ISBN 978-

1-4263-0844-4 LE ISBN 978-1-4263-0845-1. Illustrated by Christina Balit. Napoli follows Greek mythology's evolution from its creation story and elemental early deities to the psychologically resonant lives of later heroes. Her language is animated and thoughtful, her characters fully equipped with histories and emotions that propel their behavior. Twenty-five deities and mortals get full chapters that include Balit's gloriously star-spangled double page–spread portraits—boldly expressive, large-eyed, muscled figures in a handsome saturated palette. Reading list, timeline, websites. Bib., ind.
Folktales/Myths/and Legends; Mythology, Greek

Reinhart, Matthew and Sabuda, Robert. Encyclopedia Mythologica: Dragons & Monsters. 12 pp. Candlewick 2011. ISBN 978-0-7636-3173-4.
Reinhart and Sabuda divide the wonderful world of dragons and monsters into six major categories, creating a glorious double-page pop-up for each. Not a millimeter of space is wasted; the pop-ups easily fold inside themselves and each spread additionally contains a series of foldout mini-books. The text, often showing humor, acts as extended captions for the illustrations.
Folktales/Myths/and Legends; Dragons; Monsters; Toy and movable books

Rylant, Cynthia. The Beautiful Stories of Life: Six Greek Myths, Retold. 73 pp. Harcourt (Harcourt Trade Publishers) 2009. ISBN 978-0-15-206184-5. Illustrated by Carson Ellis. Using a blend of storytelling and overt interpretation, Rylant presents six myths. Her language is economical and straightforward; her tone is tenderly melancholic, softening the stories' visceral passions. Most notable is the authoritative, all-knowing narrator, whose observations direct readers' sense of the tales' meanings. Soft pencil drawings bedeck this elegant-looking little book with visions of flowers, garlands, and comely maidens.
Folktales/Myths/and Legends; Mythology, Greek

Singh, Rina. Guru Nanak: The First Sikh Guru. 64 pp. Groundwood (House of Anansi Press) 2011. ISBN 978-0-88899-958-0. Illustrated by Andrée Pouliot.
Sikhism's founder (1469–1539) was a fine poet and tradition-challenging philosopher whose principles were notably monotheistic and caste free: "Worship one God, treat everyone [including women] equally...share with the less fortunate." The dozen stories here illuminate such ideas while recounting Nanak's legendary life, starting with his laughter at birth. Pouliot's gouache and watercolor art, recalling traditional Indian illustrations, completes an attractive introduction to Sikhism.
General Religion; Biographies; Religion–Sikhism; Nanak, Guru; Poets

—FOCUS ON—

Greek Mythology

OMGS!

By Joy Fleishhacker

*Joy Fleishhacker is a librarian and a freelance editor
and writer who lives in Colorado.*

Terrifying monsters and fearsome beasts? Courageous and quick-witted heroes? Thrilling adventures and dangerous quests? These tales have it all, plus the unforgettable characters, timeless themes, and range of human emotion that have drawn people to Greek myths for eons. Included here is a spectacular array of offerings guaranteed to tempt myriad tastes and reading abilities presented in user-friendly sections: picture books, inviting collections of tales each with a unique approach and style of artwork, graphic novels, novel-length recountings or imaginative reinterpretations, and browser-tempting guidebooks. Assuming that tried-and-true titles such as *D'Aulaires' Book of Greek Myths* (Delacorte, 1992) and Rosemary Sutcliff's works still grace your shelves, this list showcases newer books that represent a variety of formats and storytelling approaches. For the most part, the focus is on traditional stories set in ancient times (sorry, Percy Jackson) though many of the tellings have a modern-day flair, and all appeal to 21st-century sensibilities.

Educators will find much inspiration here for classroom explorations, as these books are ideal for introducing the Greek pantheon, launching discussions of literary genres, and forging links to other areas of the curriculum, including history, culture, and art. Contrast different authors' takes on these well-known characters and tales, and talk about how a book's format, illustrations, and narrative tone affect each interpretation. Take a pop-culture approach and make comparisons between today's comic-book-based superheroes and their just-as-amazing ancient antecedents and help your students ascertain why hero tales remain storytelling staples. Share these books with students and tempt them into a world of wonders that will amuse, amaze, entertain, and inform.

PICTURE BOOKS

Byrd, Robert. The Hero and the Minotaur: The Fantastic Adventures of Theseus. illus. by author. Dutton. 2005. RTE $17.99. ISBN 978-0-525-47391-6.

Gr 3-6–Masterfully intertwining several myths, Byrd presents a drum-tight recounting of the quick-witted Theseus's exploits as he journeys to meet his royal father, routs a trio of giant-size rogues, and vows to vanquish the dreaded "half-man, half-bull" monster. A tale of triumph and tragedy, splendidly illustrated with sun-drenched paintings steeped in classical motifs.

Clayton, Sally Pomme. Persephone. illus. by Virginia Lee. Eerdmans. 2009. Tr $18. ISBN 978-0-8028-5349-3.

Gr 3-6–When Persephone is "plucked" from a flower-filled field by Hades and carried off to the Underworld, a distraught Demeter mourns for her daughter, and the very Earth feels the effects. Imagery and detail in the lyrical language and terracotta-toned paintings eloquently convey this beguiling tale's deep-felt emotion and enduring circle-of-life themes.

Harris, John. Strong Stuff: Herakles and His Labors. illus. by Gary Baseman. Getty. 2005. Tr $16.95. ISBN 978-0-892-36784-9. LC 2004007904.

Gr 2-6–From vanquishing the Nemean Lion to rounding up the Golden Apples, this exuberant picture book recounts Herakles's "super-difficult jobs" with campy humor and visual élan. Depicting a brawny hero sporting a loincloth, lace-up sandals, and perpetual five-o'clock shadow, Baseman's revved-with-colors cartoon artwork is a perfect fit for Harris's tongue-in-cheek text.

Karas, G. Brian. Young Zeus. illus by author. Scholastic. 2008. Tr $16.95. ISBN 978-0-439-72806-5. LC 2009010148.

Gr 2-6–In this spirited imagining of the all-powerful god's early days, Zeus leaves behind an idyllic boyhood to defeat his fearsome father, release his swallowed-down siblings, conquer the Titans, and assume his place as "boss" of Mount Olympus. This accessible tale is illustrated with dynamic earth-toned artwork and infused with a play-ful childlike perspective. Audio version available from Recorded Books.

O'Malley, Kevin. Mount Olympus Basketball. illus. by author. Walker. 2003. RTE $16.85. ISBN 978-0-802-78845-0; pap $6.95. ISBN 978-0-802-77728-7.
Gr 2-6–The Gods (including a smugly smiling Zeus and a rough-and-tumble Athena) take on the Mortals (captained by a hearty Hercules) in a "Mediterranean meltdown" on the court. Color-saturated cartoon artwork depicts the hilarious slam-dunking, el-bows-flying action while two sportscasters provide the droll play-by-play—along with fun-to-follow-up-on allusions to many well-known myths.

COLLECTED TALES

Kimmel, Eric A. The McElderry Book of Greek Myths. il-lus. by Pep Montserrat. S & S/McElderry. 2008. RTE $21.99. ISBN 978-1-4169-1534-8.
K-Gr 5–From "Prometheus" to "Perseus and Medusa," Kimmel presents 12 favorite legends, streamlining events into selections concise enough to share with a class and enticing enough to whet appetites for more. Blending ancient motifs and patterns with modern-looking textures and hues,

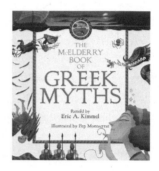

the stylized paintings grandly depict characters both mortal and divine.

Lunge-Larsen, Lise. Gifts from the Gods: Ancient Words & Wisdom from Greek & Roman Mythology. illus. by Gareth Hinds. Houghton Harcourt. 2011. RTE $18.99. ISBN 978-0-547-15229-5.
Gr 3-7–Mixing mythology and etymology, Lunge-Larsen introduces 17 "ancient words" derived from classical characters. From "Achilles' Heel" to "Victory," the terms and their tales are presented in vividly written, handsomely illustrated entries. Ideal for classroom sharing, this unique offering can launch discussion about the power of story and its influence on modern-day language.

Napoli, Donna Jo. Treasury of Greek Mythology: Classic Stories of Gods, Goddesses, Heroes & Monsters. illus. by Christina Balit. National Geographic. 2011. Tr $24.95. ISBN 978-1-4263-0844-4; PLB $33.90. ISBN 978-1-4263-0845-1.
Gr 5 Up–Wise, witty, worldly, and thoroughly entrancing, this collection presents 25 tales showcasing the Greek pantheon's major players. At once eloquent and el-

emental, poetic and contemporary, these deftly written selections gloriously regale the characters' legendary adventures while vivifying them with personality. Balit's stunning paintings feature luminous colors, rich patterns, and star-infused motifs.

Rylant, Cynthia. The Beautiful Stories of Life: Six Greek Myths, Retold. illus. by Carson Ellis. Harcourt. 2009. Tr $18. ISBN 978-0-15-206184-5.
Gr 6-9–Writing with an eye toward the grand spectrum of the human experience, Rylant introduces readers to Pandora, Persephone, Orpheus, Pygmalion, Narcissus, and Psyche. Themes of love, sacrifice, forgiveness, and courage are presented with quiet wisdom, honest emotion, and a touch of romance. Ellis's sophisticated, soft-edged illustrations echo the text's intimate tone. Audio version available from Recorded Books.

Townsend, Michael. Amazing Greek Myths of Wonder and Blunders. illus. by author. Dial. 2010. Tr $14.99. ISBN 978-0-8037-3308-4; ebook $12.99. ISBN 978-1-1011-9557-4.
Gr 3-8–Townsend reels out comic-book-style renditions of nine legends including "Pygmalion and His Rocky Relationship," "Arachne Gets a Big Head," and "The Short Flight of Icarus," eye-poppingly illustrated with neon-bright cartoons. Abounding with zany antics, clever reinterpretations of familiar tropes, and 21st-century tweaks, these riotous retellings will wow readers while conveying the essence of the originals.

Turnbull, Ann. Greek Myths. illus. by Sarah Young. Candlewick. 2010. Tr $18.99. ISBN 978-0-763-65111-4.
Gr 4-8–Divided into three thematic sections, Turnbull's articulate retellings of 16 tales flow lyrically from one to the next, helping readers to make connections (e.g., "The Minotaur" is followed by "Ariadne on Naxos"). Young's opulent mixed-media artwork balances tantalizing textures with formal-looking figures to add detail and enhance the mood of majesty and wonder. Audio version available from Brilliance Audio.

Williams, Marcia. Greek Myths for Young Children. illus. by author. Candlewick. 1992. RTE $17.99. ISBN 978-1-564-02115-1; pap $8.99. ISBN 978-0-763-65384-2.
Gr 1-6–Eight tales featuring non-divine protagonists (Pandora, Orpheus, etc.) are retold in color-saturated kid-pleasing comic strips. Williams doesn't shy away from the violence inherent in these stories, but her knack for interjecting bawdy visual humor or an offbeat dialogue-balloon aside maintains a buoyant tone. The

intricate artwork and pithy narratives demand repeated readings and guarantee wide appeal.

GRAPHIC NOVELS

Ford, Christopher. Stickman Odyssey: An Epic Doodle. Bk. 1. illus. by author. Philomel. 2011. Tr $12.99. ISBN 978-0-399-25426-0.

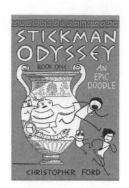

Gr 5-9–Banished from Sticatha by an evil witch, "far-wandering" Zozimos embarks on a voyage home filled with heroic battles, manic monsters, and heaps of irreverent humor. Ford's lithe-lined stick-figure characters run amok in a tale that incorporates a mishmash of myths, a delightfully meandering plot, and a tempting taste of the real McCoy.

Mucci, Tim, adapt. The Odyssey. Bk. 3. illus. by Ben Caldwell & Rick Lacy. (All-Actions Classics Series). Sterling. 2010. pap $7.99. ISBN 978-1-4027-3155-6.
Gr 6 Up–Concise and briskly paced, this dynamic comic-book version streamlines Homer's plot and zooms in on the all-out monster-trouncing, enchantress-encountering, death-defying action. The exploits of the square-jawed Odysseus are resplendent in bold lines and jewel tones while the fickle gods and goddesses shimmer in translucent hues. A reader-grabbing intro to the epic.

O'Connor, George. Athena: Grey-Eyed Goddess. Bk. 2. 2010. ISBN 978-1-59643-649-7; ISBN 978-1-59643-432-5.
——.Hera: The Goddess and Her Glory. Bk. 3. 2011. ISBN 978-1-59643-724-1; ISBN 978-1-59643-433-2.
——.Zeus: King of the Gods. Bk. 1. 2010. ISBN 978-1-59643-625-1; ISBN 978-1-56943-431-8.
ea. vol: illus. by author. (Olympians Series). First Second. Tr $16.99; pap. $9.99.
Gr 5 Up–These riveting graphic novels balance carefully researched retellings with strong characterizations, satisfying humor, and superhero-style action. Stunning artwork and compelling scripts relate five thrilling stories about the headstrong Athena; provide fresh perspective on Hera and her role in the fraught-with-trials tale of Heracles; and introduce world-shaking Zeus, from sheltered boyhood to Titan-toppling mêlées to ascendance to the throne. Look for the other titles in this series.

Storrie, Paul D. Perseus: The Hunt for Medusa's Head. illus. by Thomas Yeates. (Graphic Myths and Legends Series). Graphic Universe/Lerner. 2008. PLB $27.93. ISBN 978-0-822-57528-3; pap. $8.95. ISBN 978-1-580-13888-8.

Gr 4-8–Beginning with a visit from Athena, who bestows upon the troubled hero magical gifts and a sense of hope for completing his "terrible task," this gripping graphic novel relates Perseus's ancestry and his spine-tingling adventures via concise dialogue and packed-with-kapow artwork. Check out other entries in the series for first-rate renditions sure to captivate comics fans.

NOVELS

Collins, Ross. Medusa Jones. illus. by author. Scholastic/Arthur A. Levine. 2008. RTE $16.99. ISBN 978-0-439-90100-0. LC 2007017199.

Gr 3-5–Snake-haired Medusa and her best buddies—a centaur and a minotaur—are constantly picked on by Acropolis Academy's popular crowd, but when disaster strikes during a school trip, the "freaks" prove that they are truly heroes. This fast-reading romp features sprightly sketches, snicker-inducing humor, and timeless issues of self-image and bullying.

Cooney, Caroline B. Goddess of Yesterday: A Tale of Troy. Delacorte. 2002. Tr $15.95. ISBN 978-0-385-72945-1; PLB $17.99. ISBN 978-0-385-90051-5; pap. $8.99. ISBN 978-0-385-73865-1; ebook $8.99. ISBN 978-0-307-48549-6.

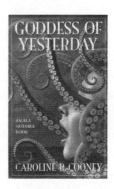

Gr 5-8–After Siphnos is sacked by pirates, 12-year-old Anaxandra takes on the identity of Callisto, the princess for whom she had served as companion, and soon finds herself before a ruthless Helen as the tragic events of the Trojan War unfold. Cooney places a believably created fictional character in the heart of a well-known tale. Audio version available from Recorded Books.

Friesner, Esther. Nobody's Princess. (Princesses of Myth Series). Random. 2007. Tr $16.99. ISBN 978-0-375-87528-1; PLB $18.99. ISBN 978-0-375-97528-8; pap. $7.99. ISBN 978-0-375-87529-8; ebook $3.99. ISBN 978-0-375-84984-8.

Gr 6-9–Harking back to the girlhood of Helen of Troy, Friesner introduces a tomboyish teen more interested in warrior training than feminine pastimes. The protagonist's adventure puts her alongside famed heroes while winning over readers with her free-spirited nature. The page-turning escapades continue in *Nobody's Prize* (2008) as a disguised Helen joins the quest for the Golden Fleece.

J
Fic

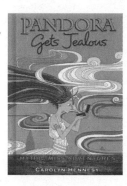

Hennesy, Carolyn. Pandora Gets Jealous. (Mythic Misadventures Series). Bloomsbury. 2008. Tr $12.95. ISBN 978-1-59990-196-1; pap. $6.99. ISBN 978-1-59990-291-3. LC 2007023975.

Gr 5-8–When the box that Pandy has brought to Athena Maiden Middle School for her annual project accidently opens, releasing seven great plagues, a furious Zeus insists that she round them up. Helped by her two BFFs, she sets out to save the world and find her place in it. Hennesy reinterprets the myth with humor and present-day panache. The quest continues in *Pandora Gets Vain* (2008), *Pandora Gets Lazy* (2009), and *Pandora Gets Heart* (2010), and several additional titles.

J
Fic

Holub, Joan & Suzanne Williams. Athena the Brain. Bk. 1. ISBN 978-1-4169-8271-5; ISBN 978-1-4169-9912-6. LC 2009019170.
——. Persephone the Phony. Bk. 2. ISBN 978-1-4169-8272-2; ISBN 978-1-4169-9913-3. LC 2009019176.
ea. vol: (Goddess Girls Series). S & S/Aladdin. 2010. pap. $5.99; ebook $5.99.

Gr 3-6–Mythology meets middle-school angst as preteen "goddess girls" navigate the ups and downs of social life at Mount Olympus Academy. New student Athena can't wait to rise to fresh challenges but must first deal with the ultimate mean-girl, Medusa; all-too-agreeable Persephone finds herself "going along to get along" until she meets school bad boy Hades. Contemporary concerns are cleverly interwoven into the Greek pantheon in these frothy, funny fantasies.

J
MP3

Mccaughrean, Geraldine, retel. Hercules. (Heroes Series). Cricket. 2005. Tr $17.95. ISBN 978-0-812-62737-4.

Gr 5-9–The action launches with a memorable moment—baby Hercules effortlessly dispatching two deadly snakes in his cradle—and never slows down as the ill-fated hero atones for an impetuous act by attempting 12 seemingly impossible tasks. Starring a multidimensional protagonist, this spellbinding novelization zings with vividly delineated daredevil deeds and lyrical language. Steer fans toward the author's equally scintillating *Odysseus* (2004), *Perseus* (2005), and *Theseus* (2005). Audio version available from Full Cast Audio.

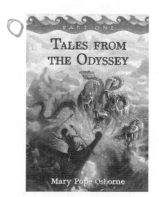

Osborne, Mary Pope. Tales from the Odyssey: Part One. ISBN 978-1-423-12864-9.

——. Tales from the Odyssey: Part Two. ISBN 978-1-423-12610-2.

ea. vol: illus. by Troy Howell. Hyperion. 2010. pap. $5.99. Gr 3-6–Colorfully adorned with reader-grabbing covers, these two volumes collect all six installments of Osborne's thrilling chapter-book series about this lauded-by-Homer hero and his far-flung adventures. Straight-arrow plotting, simply phrased yet elegantly crafted language, and supercharged suspense make for a first-rate read-aloud or read-alone introduction to the epic.

GUIDEBOOKS

Bryant, Megan E. Oh My Gods!: A Look-It-Up Guide to the Gods of Mythology. ISBN 978-1-60631-026-7; ISBN 978-1-60631-058-8. LC 2009017169.

——. She's All That!: A Look-It-Up Guide to the Godesses of Mythology. ISBN 978-1-60631-027-4; ISBN 978-1-60631-059-5. LC 2009017168.

Kelly, Sophia. What a Beast!: A Look-It-Up Guide to the Monsters and Mutants of Mythology. ISBN 978-1-60631-028-1; ISBN 978-1-60631-028-3.

Otfinoski, Steven. All in the Family: A Look-It-Up Guide to the In-laws, Outlaws, and Offspring of Mythology. ISBN 978-1-60631-025-0; ISBN 978-1-60631-057-1. LC 2009020999.

ea. vol: (Mythlopedia Series). Watts. 2009. PLB $39.; pap. $13.95. Gr 5-9–These A-to-Z guides to the denizens of Mount Olympus deftly sum up each figure's origins, career highlights, and associated myths. Humorous monologues, full-color reproductions of artworks

(often amusingly decorated with modern-day bling), and cheeky cartoons add to the lighthearted tone.

J
293.13
Curlee, Lynn. Mythological Creatures: A Classical Bestiary. illus. by author. S & S/Atheneum. 2008. RTE $18.99. ISBN 978-1-4169-1453-2. LC 2006016980.

Gr 3-8–Curlee introduces an array of strange beings and fearsome beasts, including Polyphemus, the Harpies, and the Chimera. Handsome portraits are paired with text that gracefully touches on the pertinent myths, fueling further reading.

Smith, Charles R. The Mighty 12: Superheroes of Greek Myth. illus. by P. Craig Russell. Little, Brown. 2008. Tr $16.99. ISBN 978-0-316-01043-6

Gr 5-8–Comic-book artwork and vigorous rap-style rhymes highlight each Olympian's attributes and realm of power. The text regales aspects both heroic and terrifying as a furious Poseidon crumbles buildings and a jealous Hera proves "that the goddess supreme/can be the cold-hearted/queen of mean." Punch-packing spreads portray appropriately idealized immortals and nasty-looking creatures.

ON THE WEB

For Teachers

Windows to the Universe: Mythology. www.windows2universe.org/mythology/mythology.html. National Earth Science Teachers Association. (Accessed 12/9/13).
Emphasizing "the historical and cultural ties between science, exploration, and the human experience," this site introduces ancient deities and myths and their association with aspects of the Earth, sky, and physical world (constellations, planets, etc.). The text is written for three reading levels (changed via tab) and packed with artworks, star charts, maps, and more.

For Students

Encyclopedia Mythica: Greek Mythology. pantheon.org/areas/mythology/europe/greek. Encyclopedia Mythica. (Accessed 12/9/13).
Gr 6 Up–Clearly written, signed articles introduce the gods, heroes, and monsters

of Greek mythology. A page listing deities (and their Roman counterparts) makes for easy searching, and links within the essays allow readers to explore relationships and related tales. A solid resource for reports.

Hercules: Greece's Greatest Hero. www.perseus.tufts.edu/Herakles. Perseus Project/ Tufts University. (Accessed 12/9/13).
Gr 3 Up–From his labors to his loves, this museum-exhibit-style site introduces the life and times of Hercules. Dynamic and delightfully detailed, the content is illustrated with vibrant images painted on ancient Greek vases, photos of archae-ological sites, maps, and quotes from classical texts.

Winged Sandals. www.abc.net.au/arts/wingedsandals/default_lowband.htm. ABC (Australian Broadcasting Corporation) and the University of Melbourne. (Ac-cessed 9/19/11).
Gr 1-6–Lively, easy to navigate, and informative, this inviting site includes ani-mated versions of stories, myth-themed online games, craft projects, and histori-cal tidbits. An accessible "Who's Who" of gods, mortals, and monsters offers quick bios, family trees, descriptions of major events, and audio pronunciations.

Eds. Note: The full version of "OMGs!"
is available online at http://bit.ly/15nKlON

Science

Ancona, George. It's Our Garden: From Seeds to Harvest in a School Garden. 48 pp. Candle-wick 2013. ISBN 978-0-7636-5392-7.

From spring planting to winterization, full-color photographs chronicle a year in the life of an elementary school garden in San-ta Fe; students are shown composting soil, watering plants, and sampling the edible de-lights. While green is visually ubiquitous, the real star is the white space, which keeps each spread from becoming crowded. Ancona's

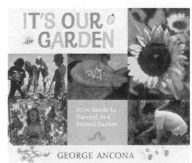

no-nonsense text is perfectly suited for newly independent readers. Websites. Bib.
*Farm Life/Husbandry/and Gardening; Schools–Elementary schools; New Mexico; Seasons;
Composts; Plants; Fruits and vegetables*

Arnold, Ann. Sea Cows, Shamans, and Scurvy: Alaska's First Naturalist: Georg Wilhelm
Steller. 227 pp. Farrar/Foster 2008. ISBN 978-0-374-39947-4.
In the 1740s, German scientist Georg Steller set out across Siberia to the Kamchatka
Peninsula and into what is now Alaska. He identified numerous animals and plants
and worked with the native people. Arnold draws mainly from Steller's journals for
her account; her sketches throughout create a sense of a field diary. The book reveals
much about early exploration and scientific study. Timeline. Bib., ind.
*Geography and Exploration; Natural history; Scientists; Naturalists; Biographies; Alaska;
Russia; Steller, Georg Wilhelm*

Arnold, Caroline. Giant Sea Reptiles of the Dinosaur Age. 40 pp. Clarion 2007. ISBN
978-0-618-50449-7. Illustrated by Laurie Caple.

Arnold interweaves data about three major reptile
groups—ichthyosaurs, plesiosaurs, and mosasaurs—
with accounts of fossil finds and theoretical advances
that helped paleontologists put together the facts upon
which the book is based. Size, eating habits, and location
are explored. Arnold's informative text is accompanied
by Caple's finely detailed illustrations of the various
creatures in action under the sea. Timeline. Ind.
*Prehistoric Life; Animals–Reptiles; Animals–Marine ani-
mals; Animals–Extinct animals; Fossils; Paleontology; Scientists*

Arnold, Caroline. Global Warming and the Dinosaurs: Fossil Discoveries at the Poles.
40 pp. Clarion 2009. ISBN 978-0-618-80338-5. Illustrated by Laurie Caple.
Arnold introduces dinosaur species that lived during the Cretaceous Period in the
polar regions, once thought too cold for dinosaur survival. After an introduction on
paleoclimatology and fossil finds, the discussion alternates between descriptions of
major species and historical accounts of scientists and fossil collectors. Caple's luminous watercolors place the dinosaurs in lush northern forests and beaches reminiscent
of today's Pacific Northwest. Websites. Ind.
*Prehistoric Life; Environment–Greenhouse effect; Global warming; Prehistoric life–Dino-
saurs; Polar regions*

J
Easy

Bang, Molly and Chisholm, Penny. Living Sunlight: How Plants Bring the Earth to Life. 40 pp. Scholastic/Blue Sky (Scholastic Trade Division) 2009. ISBN 978-0-545-04422-6. Illustrated by Molly Bang.

This account of photosynthesis is narrated by the sun. Shining on every page, it celebrates its power with bursts of bright yellow connecting with the greens of Earth. Circular paintings emphasize the continuity of nature, while the spare, poetic narrative describes the process of converting energy and carbon dioxide into sugar. Back matter gives further information about the scientific process of photosynthesis.

Natural History; Environment–Ecology; Plants; Astronomy–Sun; Photosynthesis

J
571.455

Bang, Molly and Chisholm, Penny. Ocean Sunlight: How Tiny Plants Feed the Seas. 48 pp. Scholastic/Blue Sky (Scholastic Trade Division) 2012. ISBN 978-0-545-27322-0.

This fresh perspective on food chains focuses on the critical and voluminous ocean-based plant life—plankton—and the transfer of energy and nutrients from the sun to these microscopic plants to ocean animals and back. Glowing illustrations, age-appropriate explanations, well-chosen text and visual analogies, and a series of rhetorical questions are used to excellent effect. Six pages of notes are appended.

Natural History; Biology; Food chains; Oceans; Astronomy–Sun; Photosynthesis; Plants; Animals–Marine animals

Bishop, Nic. Nic Bishop Lizards. 48 pp. Scholastic 2010. ISBN 978-0-545-20634-1 PE ISBN 978-0-545-60569-4.

Bishop provides spectacular photographic images, accompanied by excellent scientific information about the many lizard species, their behaviors, anatomy, survival mechanisms, and habitats. Brilliant color photographs bring us sharply into close-ups of the nubby texture of lizard skin or capture frame-by-frame the animals in mid-jump (most impressively across two foldout pages showing every nuance of a basilisk skimming the surface of water). Reading list. Glos., ind.

Reptiles and Amphibians; Animals–Lizards

Bishop, Nic. Nic Bishop Snakes. 48 pp. Scholastic Nonfiction 2012. ISBN 978-0-545-20638-9.

Seemingly impossible-to-get shots of snakes poised and alert, arched and ready to strike, and even swallowing an egg whole are interspersed with more restful moments during

which they are coiled onto branches or camouflaged by sand. It will take a while for readers to tear themselves away from the images to read the excellent accompanying text that describes snake behavior, physiology, and eating habits. Reading list. Glos., ind.
Reptiles and Amphibians; Animals–Snakes

Bonner, Hannah. When Fish Got Feet, Sharks Got Teeth, and Bugs Began to Swarm: A Cartoon Prehistory of Life Long before Dinosaurs. 48 pp. National (National Geographic Books) 2007. ISBN 978-1-4263-0078-3 LE ISBN 978-1-4263-0079-0 PE ISBN 978-1-4263-0546-7.

This scientifically thorough but humorous account focuses on the Silurian and Devonian periods. Bonner's friendly, engaging writing enlivens a comprehensive explanation of conceptually challenging biology; the science is first-rate. Equally effective are the multilayered cartoonlike illustrations containing cultural references for both adults and children. Most of the illustrations are not just funny but truly scientific, clarifying ideas through clever visual metaphors. Timeline, websites. Bib., glos., ind.
Prehistoric Life; Paleontology; Fossils; Animals–Extinct animals

Bradley, Timothy J. Paleo Bugs: Survival of the Creepiest. 48 pp. Chronicle 2008. ISBN 978-0-8118-6022-2.

Bradley (*Paleo Sharks*) traces the evolution of arthropods from 530 million years ago to today. With a crisp graphic format and a handsome color palette, each double-page spread includes a central illustration featuring a dramatic portrayal of several creatures (often doing battle); to-scale silhouettes of the animals and a human child; and information about present-day relatives. Reading list. Bib., glos.
Prehistoric Life; Paleontology; Fossils; Animals–Extinct animals; Animals–Arthropods

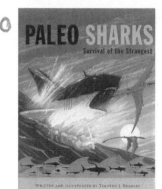

Bradley, Timothy J. Paleo Sharks: Survival of the Strangest. 48 pp. Chronicle 2007. ISBN 978-0-8118-4878-7. Bradley's chronologic tour of extinct shark species employs a smart design and sharp graphics to tie together the encyclopedia-like entries. Each two-page layout includes one or two profiles of sharks, a related text box, and a to-scale comparison. In the accompanying illustrations, sharks sport colorful stripes, spots, and other markings (though Bradley is careful to explain that these are his interpretations). Reading list. Bib., glos.
Prehistoric Life; Animals–Extinct animals; Fossils; Animals–Sharks; Paleontology

Q **Burns, Loree Griffin.** Citizen Scientists: Be a Part of Scientific Discovery from Your Own Backyard. 80 pp. Holt 2012. ISBN 978-0-8050-9062-8 PE ISBN 978-0-8050-9517-3. Photographs by Ellen Harasimowicz.

Burns brings much-deserved attention to four remarkable scientific projects that enlist regular people in data collection: the Monarch Watch butterfly tagging project, the Audubon Christmas Bird Count, a project documenting ladybug species, and a frog study. Detailed accounts of the procedures along with the handsome color photography make the idea of participation highly appealing. Bib., glos., ind.
Natural History; Animals–Butterflies; Animals–Birds; Animals–Frogs; Animals–Ladybugs

Q **Burns, Loree Griffin.** The Hive Detectives: Chronicle of a Honey Bee Catastrophe. 66 pp. Houghton (Houghton Mifflin Trade and Reference Division) 2010. ISBN 978-0-547-15231-8 PE ISBN 978-0-544-00326-2. Photographs by Ellen Harasi- mowicz. Scientists in the Field series.

In 2006–2007, a sudden drop in the number of honeybee colonies alarmed scientists. Burns tells the story as a dramatic scientific mystery, carefully leading readers through the unfolding of the crisis and attempts to solve it. Profiles of beekeepers and details about bees and honey making, along with gloriously crisp photographs, are interspersed throughout the main text. Reading list, websites. Bib., glos., ind.
Insects and Invertebrates; Scientists; Animals–Honeybees; Wildlife rescue; Animals–Bees; Beekeeping

Q **Burns, Loree Griffin.** Tracking Trash: Flotsam, Jetsam, and the Science of Ocean Motion. 58 pp. Houghton (Houghton Mifflin Trade and Reference Division) 2007. ISBN 978-0-618-58131-3 PE ISBN 978-0-547-32860-7. Scientists in the Field series.

When hundreds of sneakers washed up on the Washington coast, scientist Curt Ebbesmeyer discovered that they came from a cargo spill, and he began studying the Pacific Ocean's currents. Burns's book conveys solid scientific explanations of ocean patterns and discusses the tracking of debris and the effect of ocean trash on the environment. Scientific information builds, creating a natural detective story. Reading list, websites. Bib., glos., ind.
General Science and Experiments; Oceans; Environment–Refuse and refuse disposal; Environment–Ecology; Environment–Pollution

○ **Carson, Mary Kay.** The Bat Scientists. 80 pp. Houghton (Houghton Mifflin Trade and Reference Division) 2010. ISBN 978-0-547-19956-6 PE ISBN 978-0-544-10493-8. Photographs by Tom Uhlman. Scientists in the Field series.

With deft description and careful explanation, Carson profiles Bat Conservation International (BCI) as it researches the misunderstood title creatures. Clear text debunks "Batty Myths"—bats aren't flying mice nor do they suck blood—as it highlights BCI's conservation efforts. Uhlman's large photos are not for the squeamish, but many of his shots have a stately beauty. Reading list, websites. Glos., ind.

Mammals; Animals–Bats; Scientists

○ **Carson, Mary Kay.** Emi and the Rhino Scientist. 64 pp. Houghton (Houghton Mifflin Trade and Reference Division) 2007. ISBN 978-0-618-64639-5 PE ISBN 978-0-547-40850-7. Photographs by Tom Uhlman. Scientists in the Field series.

Terri Roth, director of the Cincinnati Zoo's Center for Conservation and Research of Endangered Wildlife, and pregnant rhinoceros Emi introduce readers to the practices of captive breeding programs. Carson provides fascinating details about painstaking observational research and the creative ways scientists like Roth solve problems. Photographs featuring Roth at work are upstaged only by those of the rhinos themselves. Reading list, websites. Glos., ind.

Mammals; Zoos; Environment–Endangered species; Scientists; Animals–Rhinoceroses; Women–Scientists; Ohio; Animals–Zoo animals

J 598.07 **Cate, Annette LeBlanc.** Look Up!: Bird-Watching in Your Own Backyard. 64 pp. Candlewick 2013. ISBN 978-0-7636-4561-8.

The book starts by encouraging children to sharpen their awareness of their surroundings and to notice the presence of birds in pastoral and urban settings. Next are the basics of bird identification, then it's on to habitat, range, and migration. The discussion is lighthearted; Cate and the birds, portrayed in illustrations with speech balloons, poke fun at themselves as they teach bird observation. Bib., ind.

Birds; Bird watching

○ **Cherry, Lynne and Braasch, Gary.** How We Know What We Know About Our Changing Climate: Scientists and Kids Explore Global Warming. 66 pp. Dawn 2008. ISBN 978-1-58469-103-7 PE ISBN 978-1-58469-130-3.

Double-page spreads feature many research projects revealing changes in ecosystems, driving home the message that change really is occurring at an accelerated rate. Illustrations include sharp photographs of researchers and children in the field and laboratories as well as age-appropriate graphs and tables that transform observations into evidence. A strong underlying message is that kids can make a difference. Reading list, websites. Ind.

Pollution and Conservation; Scientists; Environment–Greenhouse effect; Global warming

Chin, Jason. Coral Reefs. 40 pp. Roaring Brook/Flash Point/Porter 2011. ISBN 978-1-59643-563-6.

Chin's text is a straightforward description of corals, their growth into reefs, and interesting inhabitants; his illustrations show a girl in the library pulling out this very book and embarking on an adventure where the contents come to life. Detailed pictures capture the dappled light of shallow water and the bright tropical colors and patterns in the featured flora and fauna.

Natural History; Books and reading; Biomes; Oceans; Coral reefs and islands; Libraries; Animals–Marine animals

Chin, Jason. Island: A Story of the Galápagos. 32 pp. Roaring Brook/Porter 2012. ISBN 978-1-59643-716-6.

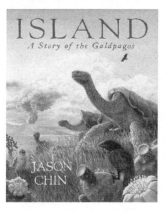

Readers witness the six-million-year development of classic biogeography example the Galápagos. The organizational structure—five chronological chapters—echoes the story line and underscores the ecological message. Gorgeous illustrations include sweeping double-page spreads and panels arranged to show dynamic changes (e.g., species adaptation). Back matter addresses natural selection, volcano formation/plate tectonics, and endemic species. An author's note discusses scientific facts versus speculation.

General Science and Experiments; Darwin, Charles; Natural disasters–Volcanoes; Evolution; Earth science; Natural history; Galápagos Islands; Islands and island life; Earth science–Plate tectonics

Chin, Jason. Redwoods. 40 pp. Roaring Brook/Flash Point/Porter 2009. ISBN 978-1-59643-430-1.

In a fantastical visual narrative paired with a straightforward nonfiction text, a young boy waiting for a subway train finds an abandoned book about redwood trees. When he exits the subway, he finds himself in the middle of a redwood forest, learning all manner of things about them. Chin's watercolors capture both the majesty of the redwoods and the young boy's inquisitive personality.

Natural History; Imagination; Trees; Books and reading; Vehicles–Subways

J
9 2

Christensen, Bonnie. I, Galileo. 40 pp. Knopf (Random House Children's Books) 2012. ISBN 978-0-375-86753-8 LE ISBN 978-0-375-96753-5.

More straightforward if less individual than Peter Sis's *Starry Messenger*, this is an excellent introduction to the scientist. The illustrations not only give geographical and historical context for Galileo's ideas and experiments but also convey the arc of the narrative. Diagrams illustrating some of Galileo's key concepts are clear and executed in a harmonious style. Bib., glos., ind.

Individual Biographies; Scientists; Physics; Italy; Astronomy; Galileo

Collard, Sneed B., III. Pocket Babies and Other Amazing Marsupials. 72 pp. Darby Creek 2007. ISBN 978-1-58196-046-4.

The book opens with detailed explanations of the geographic distribution of marsupial species, scientific classification, and the key features that make marsupials distinct from other mammals. It continues with a tour of all marsupial families, concentrating on Australasia. Collard skillfully highlights significant behaviors or physical features that are adeptly captured in the sharp-focused photographs. Conservation issues are also addressed. Reading list, websites. Bib., glos., ind.

Mammals; Animals–Marsupials; Environment–Conservation–Wildlife

Collard, Sneed B., III. Science Warriors: The Battle Against Invasive Species. 48 pp. Houghton (Houghton Mifflin Trade and Reference Division) 2008. ISBN 978-0-618-75636-0. Scientists in the Field series.

Collard profiles scientists battling two invaders causing ecological devastation: red imported fire ants in Texas and Florida's Melaleuca tree. The clear and helpful photographs show the scientists working in field and laboratory settings, as well as the featured plants and animals. Collard includes steps readers can take to help fight invasive species and a call for more public funding to fight invaders. Websites. Glos., ind.

Natural History; Scientists; Trees; Animals–Ants; Florida; Texas; Environment–Ecology

① D'Agnese, Joseph. Blockhead: The Life of Fibonacci. 40 pp. Holt 2010. ISBN 978-0-8050-6305-9. Illustrated by John O'Brien.

D'Agnese presents an engaging, kid-friendly look at Leonardo Fibonacci and his eponymous numerical sequence. In Pisa, Italy, in 1178, a young Leonardo daydreams about "the glory of numbers." But his mathematical musings lead to trouble. O'Brien's illustrations are textured with swirls and spirals—a whimsical homage to the man who discovered, as he believed, "the numbers Mother Nature uses to order the universe."

Individual Biographies; Fibonacci, Leonardo; Mathematics; Italy

J
3 63.73 **David, Laurie and Gordon, Cambria.** The Down-to-Earth Guide to Global Warming. 112 pp. Scholastic/Orchard (Scholastic Trade Division) 2007. PE ISBN 978-0-439-02494-5.

David and Gordon speak plainly and clearly to their young audience using kid-friendly metaphors. The layout makes use of color, various fonts, photographs, line drawings, charts, and maps not only to convey information but also to emphasize important points. Recommended actions are feasible: write your mayor, turn off surge protectors, get parents to buy post-consumer paper goods. Solid documentation is appended. Reading list, websites. Bib., glos., ind.

Pollution and Conservation; Environment–Greenhouse effect; Global warming; Environment–Ecology; Science

◌ Davies, Nicola. Deadly!: The Truth About the Most Dangerous Creatures on Earth. 64 pp. Candlewick 2013. ISBN 978-0-7636-6231-8. Illustrated by Neal Layton.

No punches are pulled here—this is gory-but-fascinating information about predators and prey and the adaptations that assist in their survival. Davies commendably balances spectacle and science with rich factual detail and admiration for the diversity and realities of life. Layton's cartoon illustrations skillfully lighten the tone, as animals in the throes of death or dismemberment often provide humorous asides and jokes.

Natural History; Animal defenses; Animals; Animal behavior

J
591.4 **Davies, Nicola.** Just the Right Size: Why Big Animals Are Big and Little Animals Are Little. 64 pp. Candlewick 2009. ISBN 978-0-7636-3924-2 PE ISBN 978-0-7636-5300-2. Illustrated by Neal Layton.

Davies considers the physics of anatomical structures, comparing humans' capabilities to those of smaller animals such as flies and geckos; the discussion then turns to what happens on the cellular level. Layton's cartoon illustrations are an excellent

complement to the text, assisting in the visualization of the mathematical relation-ships and also adding humor with anthropomorphized animals and cells. Glos., ind.
Natural History; Size; Animals

Davies, Nicola. Talk, Talk, Squawk!: A Human's Guide to Animal Communication. 64 pp. Candlewick 2011. ISBN 978-0-7636-5088-9 PE ISBN 978-1-4063-3854-6. Illustrated by Neal Layton.

Davies presents the ways in which animals communicate through the use of color and pattern recognition, smells, sounds, and chemical exchanges; she also discusses how humans are researching all this. Her friendly tone makes the com-plex ideas remarkably clear and understandable, and Layton's cartoon illustra-tions, complete with humorous communications from the anthropomorphized creatures, neatly underscore the important scientific messages.
Natural History; Animal communication

Davies, Nicola. What's Eating You?: Parasites—The Inside Story. 64 pp. Candlewick 2007. ISBN 978-0-7636-3460-5 PE ISBN 978-0-7636-4521-2. Illustrated by Neal Layton.

Davies states, "there are more than 430 different kinds of parasites that can live on a human body...or in one," then presents examples. What makes the often-gory de-tails easier to stomach are Davies's accessible, pun-filled explanations of the science and Layton's cartoon illustrations, which use anthropomorphism to great effect. Even readers who are a mite squeamish may be sucked in. Glos., ind.
Natural History; Microbiology

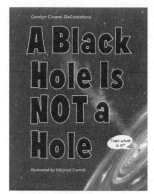

DeCristofano, Carolyn Cinami. A Black Hole Is NOT a Hole. 75 pp. Charlesbridge 2012. ISBN 978-1-57091-783-7. Illustrated by Michael Carroll.

In this captivating book on black holes, complicat-ed abstract ideas are logically ordered and clarified in an inviting conversational style and with inspired uses of reasoning and analogies perfectly attuned to the target audience. Well-designed layouts include illustrations, historical images, helpful diagrams, and humorous text bubbles that add levity while under-scoring major concepts. Timeline. Bib., glos., ind.
Astronomy; Astronomy–Black holes

Delano, Marfé Ferguson. Earth in the Hot Seat: Bulletins from a Warming World. 64 pp. National (National Geographic Books) 2009. ISBN 978-1-4263-0434-7 LE ISBN 978-1-4263-0435-4.

Delano's well-written narrative starts with examples of changes seen by scientists (shrinking glaciers, changing animal migration) then moves to thorough explanations of the underlying science. Subsequent chapters consider ecological consequences of climate change and steps humans can take to reduce the impact of excessive energy consumption. Informative captions accompany photographs illustrating the results of global warming around the planet. Reading list. Bib., ind.

Pollution and Conservation; Global warming; Environment–Greenhouse effect

Frydenborg, Kay. Wild Horse Scientists. 80 pp. Houghton (Houghton Mifflin Trade and Reference Division) 2012. ISBN 978-0-547-51831-2 PE ISBN 978-0-544-25746-7. Scientists in the Field series.

Researchers are attempting to control the horse population on Assateague Island by determining the sustainable number of horses and then developing a contraceptive vaccine that limits mares to a single foal per lifetime. The information—a combination of lab and field science details and personal observation—is accessible and engaging. Relevant and clear color photographs show both horses and scientists in situ. Reading list, websites. Bib., glos., ind.

Mammals; Animals–Horses; Environment–Conservation–Wildlife; Assateague Island National Seashore (MD and VA)

George, Jean Craighead. The Buffalo Are Back. 32 pp. Dutton 2010. ISBN 978-0-525-42215-0. Illustrated by Wendell Minor.

In George's compact ecodrama, we first see the buffalo slaughtered to decimate the Indians and open the prairie to settlers. Moving to the somber Dust Bowl migrants, we then turn to the reversal: the discovery, instigated by President Theodore Roosevelt, of three hundred remaining wild buffalo. With illustrations that both document and dramatize, it's another small triumph from a seasoned team. Websites. Bib.

Pollution and Conservation; Environment–Endangered species; Animals–Buffalo; West (U.S.); Environment–Conservation–Wildlife

Guiberson, Brenda Z.. Disasters: Natural and Man-Made Catastrophes Through the Centuries. 218 pp. Holt/Ottaviano 2010. ISBN 978-0-8050-8170-1.

Ten chapters that read like well-documented magazine articles cover a series of disasters, beginning chronologically with smallpox and concluding with Hurricane Katrina. Each opens by providing brief historical context and concludes with lasting consequences. Even though several of these catastrophes appear to be the work of nature, the careless hand of humankind is also evident. Archival photographs illustrate the events. Bib., ind.

General and World History; Disasters; Natural disasters

Harris, Robie H. It's Perfectly Normal: A Book About Changing Bodies, Growing Up, Sex, and Sexual Health. 94 pp. Candlewick 2009. ISBN 978-0-7636-4483-3 PE ISBN 978-0-7636-4484-0. Illustrated by Michael Emberley. New ed., 1994.

An unassuming, coherent, comprehensive explanation of sex in all its complicated glory. The text is freely and profusely illustrated with explicit drawings done in a frank but disarming style. All the people pictured look wonderfully happy with themselves, whether they're kissing or copulating. This fifteenth-anniversary edition has been updated with current information about issues including HIV/AIDS, HPV, and personal safety and the Internet.

Families/Children/and Sexuality; Sexuality; Human body; Babies; Pregnancy; Diseases–Sexually transmitted diseases

J 590

Hearst, Michael. Unusual Creatures: A Mostly Accurate Account of Some of Earth's Strangest Animals. 109 pp. Chronicle 2012. ISBN 978-1-4521-0467-6. Illustrated by Arjen Noordeman. Also illustrated by Jelmer Noordeman.

Field guide–like pages (including Latin names of the featured animals, habitat maps, and classification breakdowns); "Did You Know?" sidebars; and digitally colored ink drawings highlight important physiological features of fifty animals, from axolotl to yeti crab. Hearst provides many facts about the animals' appearance and behavior, and his appreciation for the quirkiness of nature shines throughout this smart, humorous volume. Ind.

Natural History

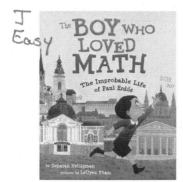

J Easy

Heiligman, Deborah. The Boy Who Loved Math: The Improbable Life of Paul Erdős. 40 pp. Roaring Brook 2013. ISBN 978-1-59643-307-6. Illustrated by LeUyen Pham.

Heiligman presents the nomadic mathematician Paul Erdős as an appealing eccentric: for instance, Paul referred to children as "epsilons" ("a very small amount in math"). Each of Pham's illustrations is a puzzle for the reader to solve, with complex numerical concepts integrated into the pictures. While the overall layout is high in appeal, the font size is too small for the target audience.

Individual Biographies; Mathematics; Erdos, Paul

Hodgkins, Fran. The Whale Scientists: Solving the Mystery of Whale Strandings. 64 pp. Houghton (Houghton Mifflin Trade and Reference Division) 2007. ISBN 978-0-618-55673-1. Scientists in the Field series.

This series entry focuses on how scientists approach the phenomenon of whale strandings. After a fascinating description of whales' evolution, the book examines humans' devastating impact on cetaceans. Hodgkins concludes with how rescuers' efforts have assisted researchers. The engagingly designed pages are enhanced by well-captioned photographs; the four chapters are subdivided to make the information-dense text manageable. Bib., glos., ind.

Mammals; Environment–Conservation–Wildlife; Scientists; Animals–Whales

Hoose, Phillip. Moonbird: A Year on the Wind with the Great Survivor B95. 148 pp. Farrar 2012. ISBN 978-0-374-30468-3.

Flying nearly from pole to pole twice a year, one robin-sized *rufa* red knot known as "Moonbird" has flown some 325,000 miles over a twenty-year lifespan. In lucid, graceful prose, Hoose details the birds' characteristics, profiles scientists and activist kids, and takes a sobering look at long-term prospects for survival. Glorious full-page and smaller photographs alternate with helpful maps in an informative progression of images. Bib., ind.

Birds; Migration; Bird watching; Environment–Conservation–Wildlife

Jackson, Donna M. Extreme Scientists: Exploring Nature's Mysteries from Perilous Places. 80 pp. Houghton (Houghton Mifflin Trade and Reference Division) 2009. ISBN 978-0-618-77706-8 PE ISBN 978-0-544-25003-1. Scientists in the Field series.

This volume profiles three stereotype-shattering scientists whose field research provides some pretty intense experiences: a meteorologist/hurricane hunter, microbiologist/caver, and ecologist/redwood climber. Jackson hits just the right balance between informative descriptions of the science and excitement surrounding the risks involved. The numerous intriguing photos achieve this balance as well, showcasing all three scientists both in the lab and out in their elements. Reading list, websites. Glos., ind.

Natural History; Scientists; Exploration and explorers

Jackson, Donna M. Phenomena: Secrets of the Senses. 175 pp. Little 2008. ISBN 978-0-316-16649-2.

Jackson moves beyond the basics of sensory perception to explore fascination with the unexplained, showing how our minds can transform sensory inputs into phenomena such as the "sixth sense" (e.g., low-frequency sounds cause us to feel uneasy in "haunted" environments). She also examines how the brain and new technologies compensate for missing senses. Black-and-white illustrations include stock photographs and scientific diagrams. Reading list, websites. Bib., glos., ind.
Medicine/Human Body/and Diseases; Senses and sensation

Jenkins, Martin. Can We Save the Tiger? 56 pp. Candlewick 2011. ISBN 978-0-7636-4909-8 PE ISBN 978-1-4063-3208-7. Illustrated by Vicky White.

This volume provides a gracefully organized overview of how some of our endangered fellow creatures are doing. Jenkins's narrative voice is engagingly informal and lucid. White's pencil and oil paint illustrations fill the large pages; the pictures are mostly in sober black and white with occasional blushes of color. A stunningly beautiful book as well as an eloquent appeal and consciousness raiser. Websites. Ind.
Pollution and Conservation; Environment–Endangered species; Animals; Environment–Conservation–Wildlife

J 595.76 Jenkins, Steve. The Beetle Book. 40 pp. Houghton (Houghton Mifflin Trade and Reference Division) 2012. ISBN 978-0-547-68084-2.

Highlighting the amazing diversity of this truly fascinating insect order, the book opens with basic beetle structure and function and then covers topics such as reproduction, feeding, communication, and defense mechanisms. Jenkins's colorful cut-paper illustrations are remarkably detailed, and the to-scale silhouettes found on the bottom of many spreads provide very helpful information on the range of beetle sizes.
Insects and Invertebrates; Animals–Beetles

J 636.7 Jenkins, Steve. Dogs and Cats. 40 pp. Houghton (Houghton Mifflin Trade and Reference Division) 2007. ISBN 978-0-618-50767-2 PE ISBN 978-0-547-85063-4.

Jenkins clearly presents scientific information in this uniquely styled flip-book comparison of dogs and cats. The extensive text and sidebars explicate characteristics, along with plenty of trivia. Muted cut-paper illustrations convey texture, color, and form. Generous

formatting leaves room for small illustrations in page corners to earmark tidbits about the opposite species. An inviting, multidimensional introduction to the pets we love.
Domestic Animals; Animals–Cats; Animals–Dogs; Pets

Jenkins, Steve. Down Down Down: A Journey to the Bottom of the Sea. 40 pp. Houghton (Houghton Mifflin Trade and Reference Division) 2009. ISBN 978-0-618-96636-3.

With his signature collage, Jenkins sinks readers from the surface of the Pacific down nearly 11,000 meters to the bottom of the Marianas Trench. On each double-page spread, several paragraphs of text explain the environmental conditions of the featured depth, as well as adaptations of the species therein. Excellent details, including additional facts and to-scale comparisons to humans, are appended.
Natural History; Animals–Marine animals; Oceans

Judge, Lita. Bird Talk: What Birds Are Saying and Why. 48 pp. Roaring Brook/Flash Point 2012. ISBN 978-1-59643-646-6.

Judge explains the ways in which birds communicate, and the reasons why they do so, with examples selected from a variety of bird species. The striking illustrations deftly portray communication as a whole-body endeavor, capturing the expressions, movements, and positions at key points in the messages that birds send within and across species. Additional facts about each species are appended. Bib., glos.
Birds; Animal communication

Kelly, Erica and Kissel, Richard. Evolving Planet: Four Billion Years of Life on Earth. 136 pp. Abrams 2008. ISBN 978-0-8109-9486-7.

From four billion years ago to today, this volume highlights key animal species. Up-to-date and comprehensive, the book covers cutting-edge scientific thought on evolution and natural history. The text preserves elements of the Field Museum exhibit on which it's based. The clean, field guide–like design features color-coded borders, which anchor readers in each period, and detailed illustrations based on scientists' best guesses. Timeline. Bib., glos., ind.
Natural History; Earth science–Geology; Paleontology; Fossils; Astronomy–Earth; Evolution; Animals–Extinct animals; Museums

Krull, Kathleen. Albert Einstein. 141 pp. Viking 2009. ISBN 978-0-670-06332-1. Illustrated by Boris Kulikov. Giants of Science series.

In this engrossing and remarkably accessible biography, Krull lingers just enough over Einstein's childhood to give readers time to connect with him; she also does an admirable job of explaining his theories. The text steers clear of hero worship, matter-of-factly describing Einstein's personal relationships. Kulikov's occasional pen-and-ink illustrations reflect the man's curiosity and imagination—and his unforgettable finger-in-a-light-socket hairstyle. Reading list, websites. Bib., ind.

Individual Biographies; Scientists; Einstein, Albert; Physics; Nobel Prize

Krull, Kathleen. Charles Darwin. 144 pp. Viking 2010. ISBN 978-0-670-06335-2. Illustrated by Boris Kulikov. Giants of Science series.
Krull makes no bones about Darwin's influence: "Publication day [for *On the Origin of Species*]…is considered the birthday of modern biology." A useful introduction previews his life and accomplishments, acquainting readers with both the man and the scientist. Krull's lively writing fleshes out these points, particularly emphasizing Darwin's uncertainty about publication. Kulikov's occasional art brings humor and drama to this brisk account. Websites. Ind.

Individual Biographies; Darwin, Charles; Scientists; Evolution

Krull, Kathleen. Marie Curie. 142 pp. Viking 2007. ISBN 978-0-670-05894-5 PE ISBN 978-0-14-241265-7. Illustrated by Boris Kulikov. Giants of Science series.
Curie's Nobel Prize–winning contributions led to revolutionary advances and paved the way for women in science. Without detracting from those accomplishments, Krull (*Isaac Newton*, *Sigmund Freud*) offers an unvarnished look at Curie's life and legacy, making scientific concepts accessible. The conversational narrative (ably assisted by Kulikov's black-and-white drawings) portrays a brilliant, driven woman with plenty of idiosyncrasies. Reading list, websites. Bib., ind.

Individual Biographies; Curie, Marie; Women–Biographies; Scientists; Women–Scientists; Chemistry; Nobel Prize

Lasky, Kathryn. Silk & Venom: Searching for a Dangerous Spider. 64 pp. Candlewick 2011. ISBN 978-0-7636-4222-8. Photographs by Christopher G. Knight.
Lasky shadows arachnologist Greta Binford as she investigates *Loxosceles* spiders. The text attentively explains the research in absorbing detail, clearly showing how each piece of data provides evidence for the species' migration and evolution. This care extends to the numerous photographs and diagrams that portray Binford's meticulous research techniques, the spiders themselves, and the people who find them fascinating. Websites. Bib., glos., ind.

Insects and Invertebrates; Animals–Spiders; Scientists; Women–Scientists

Lourie, Peter. The Manatee Scientists: Saving Vulnerable Species. 80 pp. Houghton (Houghton Mifflin Trade and Reference Division) 2011. ISBN 978-0-547-15254-7. Scientists in the Field series.
Scientists Fernando Rosas (Brazil), John Reynolds (Florida), and Lucy Keith (West Africa) investigate manatees in the field and in captivity. The text captures not only the science and politics of animal conservation but also the scientists' dedication. Telling much of the story are Lourie's many photographs of the manatees in their habitats and people interacting with the creatures. Reading list, websites. Glos., ind.
Mammals; Animals–Manatees; Scientists; Environment–Endangered species

Lourie, Peter. The Polar Bear Scientists. 80 pp. Houghton (Houghton Mifflin Trade and Reference Division) 2012. ISBN 978-0-547-28305-0. Scientists in the Field series.
Lourie takes us to Alaska to observe biologists researching a subpopulation of polar bears, then to the lab to see the care taken to properly process and store the data. Interspersed are commentaries from the project directors, who analyze the data and publicize the results. Crisp photographs convey the massive size of the animals and the details of the equipment needed to do research in such extreme conditions. Bib., glos., ind.
Mammals; Animals–Polar bears; Alaska; Global warming; Scientists; Environment–Conservation–Wildlife

Lourie, Peter. Whaling Season: A Year in the Life of an Arctic Whale Scientist. 80 pp. Houghton (Houghton Mifflin Trade and Reference Division) 2009. ISBN 978-0-618-77709-9. Scientists in the Field series.
Whale biologist Craig George works with the Inupiaq community documenting the bowhead whale population and Inupiaq hunts. Lourie conveys George's thoughts on living in such an extreme region and explains his path to becoming a biologist. Numerous photographs capture the piercing whites, grays, and blues of Alaska in the sunny spring as well as the bloody work of taking apart a whale. Reading list, websites. Glos., ind.
Mammals; Whaling; Animals–Whales; Arctic regions; Scientists; Alaska; Native Americans–North America–Inupiat

McGinty, Alice B. Darwin. 48 pp. Houghton (Houghton Mifflin Trade and Reference Division) 2009. ISBN 978-0-618-99531-8. Illustrated by Mary Azarian.
In this revealing work, readers can consider Darwin from two points of view: his own and his biographer's. The primary narrative follows the voyage of the *Beagle*,

and nearly every spread contains a parchment-like "letter" including edited portions of Darwin's own diary and letters. Azarian's watercolor-tinted woodcuts evoke naive art of the period. A brief author's note and source notes are appended. Bib.

Individual Biographies; Evolution; Voyages and travels; Scientists; Naturalists; Darwin, Charles

Markle, Sandra. Outside and Inside Woolly Mammoths. 40 pp. Walker 2007. ISBN 978-0-8027-9589-2 LE ISBN 978-0-8027-9590-8.

Markle engages readers in the scientific ideas about mammoth physiology and habitat. The book's highlight is the interaction between text and images; each excellent color photo is carefully chosen, discussed, and contrasted with others. The book ends with the provocative idea that the technology to clone woolly mammoths may not be far off. Reading list, websites. Glos., ind.

Prehistoric Life; Prehistoric life–Mammoths; Animals–Extinct animals; Fossils; Paleontology

Montgomery, Sy. Kakapo Rescue: Saving the World's Strangest Parrot. 74 pp. Houghton (Houghton Mifflin Trade and Reference Division) 2010. ISBN 978-0-618-49417-0. Photographs by Nic Bishop. Scientists in the Field series.

Montgomery and Bishop trek to Codfish Island off New Zealand's coast to bring us a marvelous account of the efforts of naturalists to save the kakapo. Montgomery's in-depth descriptions and Bishop's glorious photographs cover all aspects of the conservation effort. Layered into the account is information on New Zealand's history, its unique biodiversity, and the devastating consequences of human settlement on its fragile ecosystem. Bib., ind.

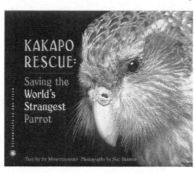

Birds; Environment–Conservation–Wildlife; Animals–Parrots; Scientists; New Zealand

Montgomery, Sy. Saving the Ghost of the Mountain: An Expedition Among Snow Leopards in Mongolia. 74 pp. Houghton (Houghton Mifflin Trade and Reference Division) 2009. ISBN 978-0-618-91645-0 PE ISBN 978-0-547-72734-9. Photographs by Nic Bishop. Scientists in the Field series.

Montgomery and Bishop (*Quest for the Tree Kangaroo*) tag along with conservationist Tom McCarthy in search of the rare snow leopard in Mongolia. Montgomery describes not just the creatures and scientists who track them but also the land and Mongolian culture. Bishop's excellent photographs feature the region's

arid, rocky landscapes, the people who live there, and the research team in action.
Mammals; Scientists; Animals–Leopards; Mongolia; Environment–Endangered species

Newquist, HP. Here There Be Monsters: The Legendary Kraken and the Giant Squid. 73
pp. Houghton (Houghton Mifflin Trade and Reference Division) 2010. ISBN
978-0-547-07678-2.

The 1860s brought a rash of sightings of enormous squidlike sea monsters. Another
wave happened in the 1960s. Photographs and video of live squid have enhanced
our understanding in recent years, but we still know little about these mysterious
creatures. The book's cover plays to the monster audience; inside, concise text, complemented by illustrations, photographs, and maps, smoothly segues between history and science. Websites. Bib., ind.
Insects and Invertebrates; Folklore–Animals; Animals–Squid; Monsters

Nivola, Claire A. Life in the Ocean: The Story of Oceanographer Sylvia Earle. 32 pp. Far-
rar/Foster 2012. ISBN 978-0-374-38068-7.

Earle's intimate knowledge of the creatures she's spent over half a century observing, whether while snorkeling near the surface or walking on the ocean floor, per-
meates this enthusiastic biography illustrated with exquisitely detailed watercolor
art. An author's note explains why we all need to get involved in efforts to curtail
the threats of overfishing, climate change, and oil spills and other pollutants. Bib.
Individual Biographies; Scientists; Oceanography; Women–Biographies; Women–Explorers;
Women–Scientists; Women–Marine biologists; Marine biology; Exploration and explorers;
Earle, Sylvia; Environment–Conservation

O'Connell, Caitlin and Jackson, Donna M. The Elephant Scientist. 71 pp. Houghton
(Houghton Mifflin Trade and Reference Division) 2011. ISBN 978-0-547-
05344-8. Photographs by Caitlin O'Connell. Scientists in the Field series.

Scientist O'Connell's contributions to our
understanding of elephant communication
propel this account. O'Connell and Jackson describe the findings in a way that lets
readers witness the unfolding of a research
program, as hypotheses lead to new insights
that beget even more questions. The many
photographs, predominantly from Namib-
ian field sites, capture the majestic elder ele-

phants, their always-appealing offspring, and dusty, rugged landscapes. Reading list, websites. Bib., glos., ind.

Mammals; Animals–Elephants; Scientists; Zoology; Women–Scientists; Women–Zoologists; Animal communication

Peterson, Brenda. Leopard & Silkie: One Boy's Quest to Save the Seal Pups. 32 pp. Holt/ Ottaviano 2012. ISBN 978-0-8050-9167-0. Photographs by Robin Lindsey.

The Seal Sitters is a Pacific Northwest watch group that educates human beach-goers and protects harbor seals when they come ashore to give birth to and care for their young. Newborn seal Leopard is fortunate to have "kid volunteer" Miles on the case. In the excellent photographs, Leopard's large, dark eyes and expressive mug seem to be smiling right at the viewer.

Mammals; Animals–Seals; Wildlife rescue; Environment–Conservation–Wildlife; Children

Pringle, Laurence. Billions of Years, Amazing Changes: The Story of Evolution. 102 pp. Boyds 2011. ISBN 978-1-59078-723-6. Illustrated by Steve Jenkins.

Pringle traces scientific developments that led to Darwin's *On the Origin of Species* as well as subsequent discoveries that have contributed to understanding of species change. Straightforward explanations of such concepts as natural selection, genetic mutations, and speciation are woven through the historical timeline, making even the most complex ideas understandable. Copious illustrations include photographs, diagrams, and Jenkins's wonderfully detailed cut-paper illustrations.

Natural History; Evolution; Darwin, Charles; Scientists

Pringle, Laurence. Penguins!: Strange and Wonderful. 32 pp. Boyds 2007. ISBN 978-1-59078-090-9 PE ISBN 978-1-62091-591-2. Illustrated by Meryl Henderson.

There's a fascination with penguins lately; in the midst of this comes Pringle's re-freshing, detailed account of penguin species—all of them, not just the one or two that typically come to mind. The clear text helps readers notice the details in Henderson's field guide–like illustrations. The book ends on a warning note about the effects of human-created pollution on penguin populations. Websites.

Birds; Animals–Penguins; Environment–Conservation–Wildlife

Ray, Deborah Kogan. Dinosaur Mountain: Digging into the Jurassic Age. 40 pp. Farrar/ Foster 2010. ISBN 978-0-374-31789-8.

Earl Douglass's expeditions in what is now Dinosaur National Monument in Colorado and Utah began in 1908 when Andrew Carnegie sent him to find "something big."

Dramatic illustrations show the land's harshness and isolation, and spot art sketching some fossil finds, tools, and preservation methods gives the book a field manual feel. Quotations from Douglass's journals indicate his reverence for the work.

Prehistoric Life; Paleontology; Fossils; Prehistoric life–Dinosaurs; Utah; Colorado; Scientists

Scott, Elaine. Mars and the Search for Life. 60 pp. Clarion 2008. ISBN 978-0-618-76695-6. Scott traces the history of our fascination with the possibility of life on Mars. She explains in detail how geologic findings could serve as evidence for the presence of water. Additional attention is focused on the challenges relating to spacecraft. Abundant color, color-enhanced, and black-and-white images give readers a feel for the Martian surface, and artistic renderings illustrate new technologies. Websites. Bib., glos., ind.

Astronomy; Astronomy–Mars; Extraterrestrial beings

Scott, Elaine. When Is a Planet Not a Planet?: The Story of Pluto. 48 pp. Clarion 2007. ISBN 978-0-618-89832-9.

The first two chapters offer information about planetary discovery. Scott then turns her attention to how scientists think, making clear the differences between hypotheses, theories, and laws. The fourth chapter outlines Pluto's planetary peculiarities. Throughout, the author reiterates that future discussions will change, because scientific knowledge is not static. Illustrations include photographs, artists' renderings, and diagrams of various planetary features. Reading list, websites. Glos., ind.

Astronomy; Astronomy–Planets; Astronomy–Pluto

Simon, Seymour. Global Warming. 32 pp. HarperCollins/Collins (HarperCollins) 2010. ISBN 978-0-06-114250-5 LE ISBN 978-0-06-114251-2 PE ISBN 978-0-06-114252-9.

With his outstandingly straightforward and logical prose, Simon leads novices through such tricky concepts as greenhouse gases and the differences between observable daily weather and long-term climate change. The book ends with the reassurance that we can help reverse the rate of change. Full-page photographs range from decorative enhancements to comparative evidence of the effects of a rise in global average temperature. Websites. Glos., ind.

Pollution and Conservation; Global warming; Environment–Greenhouse effect

Simon, Seymour. The Human Body. 64 pp. HarperCollins/Collins (HarperCollins) 2008. ISBN 978-0-06-055541-2 LE ISBN 978-0-06-055542-9.
In this survey of the twelve body systems and the senses, Simon's explanations are complemented by captivating full-page false-color images, photomicrographs, and diagrams. Simon works his usual magic to keep the narrative flowing smoothly, highlighting facts that are perfectly attuned to how young readers are both fascinated and a bit grossed out by what's inside us. Glos., ind.
Medicine/Human Body/and Diseases; Anatomy; Senses and sensation

Simon, Seymour. Our Solar System. 64 pp. HarperCollins/Collins (HarperCollins) 2007. ISBN 978-0-06-114008-2 LE ISBN 978-0-06-114009-9. New ed., 1992, Morrow.
The culmination of Simon's planets series is a fine, comprehensive work on the solar system. Similar to the others in format, the book brings together information on all the planets, a good comparison chart, and typically excellent color photographs. Beautifully designed and a pleasure to use, this edition has been updated to include new information about Pluto. Websites. Glos., ind.
Astronomy; Astronomy–Solar system

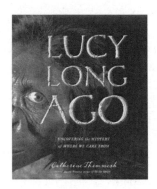

Thimmesh, Catherine. Lucy Long Ago: Uncovering the Mystery of Where We Came From. 64 pp. Houghton (Houghton Mifflin Trade and Reference Division) 2009. ISBN 978-0-547-05199-4.
Thimmesh examines the discovery of and research surrounding Lucy, the most complete early hominid skeleton found to date. The text clearly details what scientists are able to extrapolate from Lucy's bones, often by comparing them to our own skeletons and those of other primates. Explanatory sidebars, diagrams, and excellent photographs of fossils and reconstructed hominids round out this substantive package. Websites. Bib., glos., ind.
Prehistoric Life; Fossils; Paleontology; Evolution; Scientists; Anthropology

Turner, Pamela S. The Frog Scientist. 58 pp. Houghton (Houghton Mifflin Trade and Reference Division) 2009. ISBN 978-0-618-71716-3 PE ISBN 978-0-547-57698-5. Photographs by Andy Comins. Scientists in the Field series.
Readers are introduced to Dr. Tyrone Hayes, who studies the effects of pesticides on frog development. Hayes travels to a pond research site and back to his laboratory,

explaining step by step the careful procedures his team follows. Sharp, vivid photographs alternate between portrayals of the scientists—at work and relaxing—and abundant images of the frogs they study. Websites. Bib., glos., ind.

Reptiles and Amphibians; African Americans; Animals–Frogs; Scientists; Ponds

Turner, Pamela S. Life on Earth—and Beyond: An Astrobiologist's Quest. 109 pp. Charlesbridge 2008. ISBN 978-1-58089-133-2 PE ISBN 978-1-58089-134-9.

NASA scientist Chris McKay examines microbes in extreme Earth environments, gathering information about possible life in space. More than just scientific explanation, this is an in-depth look at a field scientist's adventurous career. First-rate photographs and illustrations serve mainly as a travelogue of the expeditions, though there are also telling side-by-side comparisons of arid deserts on Earth and Martian landscapes. Reading list, websites. Ind.

Astronomy; Earth science–Geology; Space; Scientists; Biomes; Biology

Turner, Pamela S. Project Seahorse. 57 pp. Houghton (Houghton Mifflin Trade and Reference Division) 2010. ISBN 978-0-547-20713-1. Illustrated by Scott Tuason. Scientists in the Field series.

Readers follow a conservation group—Project Seahorse—in its efforts to preserve seahorses, coastal reefs, and the fishing-based livelihood of the residents of Handumon, in the Philippines. Interspersed with the scientific and political work are intriguing details about seahorses, portrayed beautifully in Tuason's underwater photography. Also included are pictures of all team members—scientists and fishers alike—at work, with their families, and together celebrating their accomplishments. Reading list, websites. Glos., ind.

Pollution and Conservation; Wildlife rescue; Fishers; Animals–Sea horses; Philippines; Oceans; Animals–Marine animals; Scientists

Vogel, Carole Garbuny and Leshem, Yossi. The Man Who Flies with Birds. 64 pp. Kar-Ben 2009. ISBN 978-0-8225-7643-3.

This book describes the research of Israeli biologist Leshem, who studies the migratory patterns of raptors and other soaring birds. Vogel's well-paced text explains how Leshem became interested in bird migration and describes the tools and practices he has developed. Numerous photographs and

diagrams illustrate the migration routes and feature birds both in close-up detail and in massive migratory flocks. Reading list, websites. Ind.
Birds; Scientists; Migration; Flight; Israel

Walker, Sally M. Frozen Secrets: Antarctica Revealed. 104 pp. Carolrhoda 2010. LE ISBN 978-1-58013-607-5.
Walker investigates Antarctica's scientific mysteries. Opening with a discussion of the perilous survival conditions—from frostbite to fire—that confront modern scientists, Walker then turns her attention to the inner workings of the southernmost continent. Topics include the ubiquitous ice, Antarctica's prehistoric past, and global warming. The narrative remains lively and engaging, complemented by an array of photographs, illustrations, and maps. Reading list, websites. Bib., glos., ind.
Polar Regions; Antarctica

Webb, Sophie. Far from Shore: Chronicles of an Open Ocean Voyage. 80 pp. Houghton (Houghton Mifflin Trade and Reference Division) 2011. ISBN 978-0-618-59729-1.

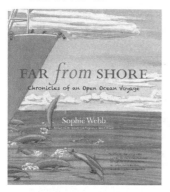

Naturalist Webb provides a richly detailed journal of her experiences as a birder on a four-month-long research cruise. The volume combines scientific information, field guide–like illustrations, and a thorough account of day-to-day life. Throughout, Webb captures the science and also the real-life minutiae of the trip. The illustrations—intricate marine-hued watercolors—take readers all over the ship and above and below the ocean. Glos., ind.
Natural History; Oceans; Animals–Marine animals; Naturalists; Voyages and travels; Scientists; Women–Scientists; Vehicles–Ships; Animals–Birds; Animals–Dolphins

Wittenstein, Vicki Oransky. Planet Hunter: Geoff Marcy and the Search for Other Earths. 48pp. Boyds 2010. ISBN 978-1-59078-592-8.
The question of life on other planets fuels this detailed examination of the work of Geoff Marcy. His research focuses on locating planets at great distances from us and determining if they resemble Earth. Wittenstein deftly captures the essence of one research community while giving attention to competing methodological approaches. The excellent color illustrations include photographs, detailed dia-

grams, and artistic renderings. Reading list, websites. Glos., ind.
Astronomy; Astronomy–Planets; Scientists; Astronomy–Earth

Yezerski, Thomas F. Meadowlands: A Wetlands Survival Story. 40 pp. Farrar 2011. ISBN 978-0-374-34913-4.

Yezerski adroitly captures the sometimes adversarial, sometimes beneficial relationship between humans and the environment in this marvelous ecological history of the Meadowlands of New Jersey. Each main double-page-spread illustration is bordered by tiny images with a wealth of additional taxonomical information (and sly humor) about the diverse flora and fauna (and mobsters and sports enthusiasts) of northern New Jersey. Websites. Bib.
Natural History; Environment–Conservation; Wetlands; New Jersey; Environment–Ecology

————————————————————————

–FOCUS ON–

Ocean Life

Going Deep

By Kathy Piehl

Kathy Piehl is Professor Emerita at Memorial Library, Minnesota State University, Mankato.

————————————————————————

In David Wiesner's *Flotsam*, a boy gazes across ocean swells while holding fantastic photos of undersea life where octopuses read by bioluminescent fish lamps and sea turtles swim with shell cities on their backs. Although the ocean covers more than 70 percent of Earth, most humans see little more than its surface, never suspecting how far down the waters extend or what fantastic plants and animals live there. Mountain ranges that dwarf Everest, trenches deeper than the Grand Canyon, and seafloor volcanoes exist in waters moving constantly in tides and currents. The titles listed here explore the marvels of this hidden world.

First up are introductions to ocean-related topics, including currents, tides, food chains, and topography. In *Down, Down, Down* and *Journey into the*

Deep, the authors organize their tours vertically, descending into ever-darker ocean zones, revealing giant tube worms and carnivorous sponges. With thousands of animals to study, most writers concentrate on a group such as whales or octopuses to show how species interact within a habitat. Books about prehistoric ocean life allow students to compare ancient animals with current ocean dwellers, while speculation about sea monsters can turn to fact as new discoveries are made.

Challenges facing scientists remain formidable. More humans have walked on the Moon than in the Marianas Trench, 35,000 feet below the surface. Although some people dive in search of sunken ships or treasure, many more study the ocean itself. The final illustration in *Life in the Ocean*, a biography of oceanographer Sylvia Earle, shows two people looking over the water. Below them, a panorama of animals and plants extends downward against deepening shades of blue. As elementary and middle school readers dive into this collection of ocean wonders, their awareness of and appreciation for the world under the sea are sure to grow.

THE BIG PICTURE

Bang, Molly & Penny Chisholm. Ocean Sunlight: How Tiny Plants Feed the Seas. illus. by Molly Bang. Scholastic. 2012. Tr $18.99. ISBN 978-0-545-27322-0.
K-Gr 4–Sunlight's role in ocean food chains extends from surface waters to pitch-black depths. The dramatic growth of phytoplankton cascading across a spread is one of many arresting illustrations, large enough for group sharing yet complex enough to study individually. Detailed notes cover topics such as photosynthesis, marine snow, and chemosynthesis.

Cole, Joanna. The Magic School Bus on the Ocean Floor. illus. by Bruce Degen. (Magic School Bus Series). Scholastic. 1992. Tr $14.99. ISBN 978-0-59041-430-2; pap. $6.99. 978-0-59041-431-9.
Gr 1-4–A diligent lifeguard tries to rescue Ms. Frizzle's class as she drives across the beach and continental shelf into deep waters. A whirlwind tour of the ocean floor and coral reefs ends with a surfboard ride to demonstrate wave action. Cartoon illustrations and fact-filled "class

report" sidebars enliven another entertaining and informative field trip. Audio and DVD versions available from Scholastic.

Green, Dan. Oceans: Making Waves! illus. by Simon Basher. (Basher Science Series). Kingfisher. 2012. Tr $14.99. ISBN 978-0-7534-6821-0. pap. $8.99. ISBN 978-0-7534-6822-7.
Gr 5-8–With its conversational tone and cartoon illustrations, this unconventional guide packs a lot of information into each double-page entry. Not only do animals introduce themselves, but ocean features such as tides, seaweed, and pollution also have their say. The wide-ranging topics and appealing format should jumpstart interest in the watery world.

J
5 91.77
Jenkins, Steve. Down, Down, Down: A Journey to the Bottom of the Sea. illus. by author. Houghton Harcourt. 2009. Tr $17. ISBN 978-0-618-96636-3.
Gr 2-6–Jenkins's masterful collages reveal characteristics of animals at different ocean depths from the sunlit surface to the deepest trench. For example, contrasting images of twilight-zone animals as they would appear in light with their glowing outlines in dark water illustrate bioluminescence. Those interested in specific species will find more information after the main text.

Johnson, Rebecca L. Journey into the Deep: Discovering New Ocean Creatures. Millbrook. 2010. PLB $31.93. ISBN 978-0-7613-4148-2.
Gr 5-8–From 2000 to 2010, hundreds of scientists worldwide participated in the Census of Marine Life. New species that they identified, such as zombie worms or yeti crabs, appear in amazing photographs that accompany quotations from scientists and descriptions of their research methods and findings at various ocean depths.

Walker, Pam & Elaine Wood. The Open Ocean. (Life in the Sea Series). Facts On File. 2005. PLB $35. ISBN 978-0-8160-5705-4.
Gr 6-10–The authors supply extensive information about the open ocean, which covers more than half of Earth's surface. Drawings and diagrams accompany clear explanations of topics such as animal anatomy, food chains, hydrothermal vents, and properties of seawater. Although a few color photos are included, the volume is aimed at researchers, not browsers.

J
Easy

Wiesner, David. Flotsam. illus. by author. Clarion. 2006. Tr $17. ISBN 978-0-618-19457-5; ebook $17. ISBN 978-0-547-75930-2.

PreS Up–Photos developed from a "Melville underwater camera" washed ashore astound the boy who discovers the device. Fantastic scenes of undersea life and images of children from years before encourage him to add his own photo to the series. Wiesner wordlessly stretches readers' imaginations about the timeless ocean circling the globe.

ANIMALS PAST AND PRESENT

Bradley, Timothy J. Paleo Sharks: Survival of the Strangest. illus. by author. Chronicle. 2007. Tr $15.95. ISBN 978-0-8118-4878-7.

Gr 4-8–Sharks from the Paleozoic, Mesozoic, and Cenozoic eras have connections to current ocean dwellers. Diagrams show relative sizes of the ancient shark, great white shark, and human diver while dramatic illustrations often feature predators and prey. Bradley clearly explains what paleontologists can and can't deduce from fossil remains.

Bulion, Leslie. At the Sea Floor Café: Odd Ocean Critter Poems. illus. by Leslie Evans. Peachtree. 2011. Tr $14.95. ISBN 978-1-56145-565-2.

Gr 5-8–Eighteen poems introduce unusual ocean animals such as the bone-eating osedax and eviscerating sea cucumbers. Linoleum-block illustrations plus fact-filled paragraphs accompany the poetic portraits. Explanations of the poetic forms, including cinquain and triolet, encourage readers to follow Bulion's lead in presenting scientific information in verse.

Buttfield, Helen. The Secret Life of Fishes: From Angels to Zebras on the Coral Reef. illus. by author. reprint ed. Diane Publishing. 2004. (original ed. Abrams, 2000). Tr $17. ISBN 978-0-7567-8075-3.

Gr 5-8–More than 250 fishes glide across the pages of this elegant introduction to life on coral reefs. Meticulous watercolor illustrations accompany Buttfield's pithy text, which often notes the importance of color and pattern for attracting mates, eluding enemies, or fooling prey. Share with students of art and design as well as ichthyologists.

Gish, Melissa. Whales. (Living Wild Series). Creative Education. 2012. PLB $35.65. ISBN 978-1-60818-084-4; pap. $8.99. ISBN 978-0-89812-676-1.

Gr 5-8–Gish packs an impressive amount of information into this well-designed volume. Effectively covering diverse science topics such as whale communication methods, life cycles, and migration patterns, she also considers whales in myth and literature and includes a Japanese fable and D. H. Lawrence poem. Large photos, maps, and illustrations will engage browsers as well.

Guiberson, Brenda Z. Into the Sea. illus. by Alix Berenzy. Holt. 1996. Tr $18.99. ISBN 978-0-8050-2263-6; pap. $8.99. ISBN 978-0-8050-6481-0.
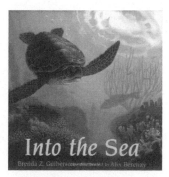
Gr 2-5–From when a hatchling makes her way across the beach until she returns to lay her eggs years later, a sea turtle lives in the ocean. Pencil and gouache illustrations depict her underwater life amid sea grass refuges and fishing net dangers. Compare this contemporary reptile with Kurt Cyrus's prehistoric *Archelon* in *The Voyage of Turtle Rex* (Harcourt, 2011).

Markle, Sandra. Octopuses. (Animal Prey Series). Lerner. 2007. PLB $25.26. ISBN 978-0-8225-6063-0; pap. $7.95. ISBN 978-0-8225-6066-1.
Gr 3-6–Octopuses must elude predators while seeking their own prey. Color photos reveal techniques such as blasting ink to distract pursuers or changing shape or color to blend in with the seafloor or reef. Views of octopuses from around the world will intrigue browsers and beginning researchers, who can follow the creatures' life cycle.

Newquist, HP. Here There Be Monsters: The Legendary Kraken and the Giant Squid. Houghton Harcourt. 2010. Tr $18. ISBN 978-0-547-07678-2.
Gr 5-8–Sailors' tales of sea monsters fueled speculation about kraken long before giant squid carcasses washed ashore in the 19th century. Illustrations range from 16th-century maps to 20th-century movie posters, accompanying summaries of legends and excerpts from poems and stories. Photos by modern scientists elucidate current research about the elusive animal.

Pfeffer, Wendy. Life in a Coral Reef. illus. by Steve Jenkins. HarperCollins. 2009. Tr $16.99. ISBN 978-0-06-029553-0; pap. $5.99. ISBN 978-0-06-445222-9.
K-Gr 3–Coral reefs bustle with activity day and night. Paper cutout illustrations capture the vibrant hues of reef animals from tiny coral polyps to a lime-green moray eel gliding past a mucus-enclosed parrot fish. Fact pages identify coral reef locations worldwide and threats to their existence.

Simon, Seymour. Coral Reefs. HarperCollins, 2013. Tr $17.99. ISBN 978-0-06-191495-9; pap. $6.95. ISBN 978-0-06-191496-6.
Gr 2-5–Vibrant close-up photos accompany Simon's informative text. He explains how coral polyps slowly develop into colonies that form different reef structures. Careful page design matches relevant photos with introductions to various hard and soft corals and unusual reef animals. Throughout, the author stresses the importance of reefs and notes threats to their survival.

Turner, Pamela S. Project Seahorse. photos by Scott Tuason. (Scientists in the Field Series). Houghton Harcourt. 2010. RTE $18. ISBN 978-0-547-20713-1.
Gr 4-8–Coral reef destruction from blast fishing, pollution, and dredging threatens many fish, including seahorses. Amazing close-up photos complement explanations of their unusual biology, including that males give birth. Attempts by Filipino scientists and villagers to establish a marine protected area demonstrate the need for cooperative conservation efforts at local, national, and international levels.

HUMAN EXPLORATIONS

Becker, Helaine. The Big Green Book of the Big Blue Sea. illus. by Willow Dawson. Kids Can. 2012. Tr $15.95. ISBN 978-1-55453-746-4; pap. $9.95. ISBN 978-1-55453-747-1.
Gr 3-6–Even students far from coastlines can participate in hands-on activities to learn about the ocean. More than 30 simple experiments employ everyday materials to investigate topics such as currents, salinity, pollution, and camouflage. Sidebars with diagrams and photos cover current issues including environmental threats and ways to help.

Berne, Jennifer. Manfish: A Story of Jacques Cousteau. illus. by Éric Puybaret. Chronicle. 2008. Tr $16.99. ISBN 978-0-8118-6063-5.
Gr 1-4–Cousteau's childhood fascination with machines, movies, and the sea provided the foundation for his inventions and explorations that drew worldwide attention to ocean life. Blue-green backgrounds painted in acrylic on linen reinforce the watery theme, especially in the fold-out panorama of Cousteau diving ever deeper. Compare this biographical introduction with Dan Yaccarino's *The Fantastical Undersea Life of Jacques Cousteau.*

Earle, Sylvia A. Dive! My Adventures in the Deep Frontier. National Geographic. 1999. RTE $18.95. ISBN 978-0-7922-7144-4.

Gr 3-7–A marine biologist, Earle shares her lifelong passion for ocean exploration and conservation. From childhood observations of creatures on shore to journeys thousands of feet below the surface in a submersible she helped design, Earle has retained her fascination with marine life. Numerous photos document various forays under the sea.

Falls, Kat. Dark Life. Scholastic. 2010. Tr $16.99. ISBN 978-0-545-17814-3; pap. $6.99. ISBN 978-0-545-17815-0.

Gr 5-9–In this futuristic novel, rising waters force humans into stack cities while pioneers farm the ocean floor. Western adventure motifs combine with subsea adaptations, such as Liquigen for breathing, as Undersea Ty and Topsider Gemma face fast-paced treachery and danger while searching for the girl's brother. Challenge readers to invent additional underwater survival strategies.

Gibbons, Gail. Sunken Treasure. illus. by author. reprint ed. HarperCollins. 1990. (original ed. Crowell, 1988). pap. $6.99. ISBN 978-0-06-446097-2.

Gr 1-4–Gibbons's exciting account of the sinking of a Spanish galleon near Florida in 1622 and the 20-year search to locate the ship more than 300 years later demonstrates that divers search for treasure as well as marine life. Detailed illustrations accompany explanations of the work involved in discovery, salvage, and restoration.

Mallory, Kenneth. Adventure Beneath the Sea: Living in an Underwater Science Station. photos by Brian Skerry. Boyds Mills. 2010. RTE $18.95. ISBN 978-1-59078-607-9.

Gr 4-8–Readers follow Mallory and Skerry through aquanaut training and their stay on Aquarius, an underwater research station. A map of Aquarius plus numerous photos give potential oceanographers insights into coral reef research as well as station life from meals to Internet connection. Mallory concludes with warnings about threats to coral reefs.

Matsen, Brad. The Incredible Record-Setting Deep-Sea Dive of the Bathysphere. Enslow. 2003. PLB $23.93. ISBN 978-0-7660-2188-4.

Gr 4-7–The 1934 dive of William Beebe and Otis Barton continues to inspire oceanographers. Diagrams of the bathysphere and period photos set the scene. Matsen effectively builds the suspense and excitement of their descent. Even though readers know the outcome, the danger surrounding the small ship in a vast ocean is palpable.

J   **Nivola, Claire A.** Life in the Ocean: The Story of Oceanographer Sylvia Earle. illus. by
5 51.   author. Farrar. 2012. Tr $17.99. ISBN 978-0-374-38068-7.
+6 69 K–Gr 3–Nivola weaves quotations from Earle into her brief biography, but richly colored illustrations draw viewers on their own. Earle swims past reef fishes, walks through bamboo coral, and plunges into a galaxy of bioluminescent creatures. The final spread incorporates earlier illustrations in a panorama of a teeming world worth exploring and preserving. Audio version available from Recorded Books.

J   **Walker, Sally M.** Secrets of a Civil War Submarine: Solving the Mysteries of the *H. L. Hun-*
973.7 *ley.* Carolrhoda. 2005. RTE $18.95. ISBN 978-1-57505-830-6.
Gr 6-10–History and science combine in a fascinating account of the submarine developed to break the Union blockade of Charleston. Documents, maps, and diagrams illustrate the Civil War section while photos enhance explanations of the 1990s work of divers, engineers, and geologists to locate and raise the *H.L. Hunley* in order to learn why she sank.

J   **Yaccarino, Dan.** The Fantastic Undersea Life of Jacques Cousteau. illus. by author. Knopf.
Fic   2009. Tr $16.99. ISBN 978-0-375-85573-3; pap.
$7.99. ISBN 978-0-375-84470-6; ebook $7.99.
ISBN 978-0-375-98755-7.

Gr 1-4–Bold colors and abstract patterns emphasize Cousteau's energetic quest to invent ways to explore the ocean, document what he saw, and share his discoveries with others. Brief quotations from Cousteau complement Yaccarino's simple text. Words are secondary to the layered illustrations, which reveal the vitality of ocean life.

ON THE WEB
For Students

The Colossal Squid. squid.tepapa.govt.nz. Museum of New Zealand Te Papa Tongarewa. (Accessed 4/22/13).
Gr 3-8–Developed in connection with the museum's exhibit of a colossal squid caught near Antarctica in 2007, this website includes photos and video clips that

show scientists at work. Interactive features allow users to descend through ocean levels to explore the squid's habitat and learn more about its anatomy.

Go with the Flow! spaceplace.nasa.gov/ocean-currents. National Aeronautics and
  Space Administration. (Accessed 4/22/13).
Gr 4-6–Video animations accompany explanations of the effects of temperature and salinity on ocean currents. An interactive game allows students to manipulate heat and salt content to change currents so their submarine can reach sunken treasure.

Marine Biology: The Living Oceans. www.amnh.org/explore/ology/marinebiology.
  American Museum of Natural History. (Accessed 4/22/13).
Gr 3-6–Whether students want to meet scientists, conduct simple experiments, or create art projects, they'll find modules that meet their interests. Interactive explorations of ocean food chains, sing-along tunes introducing bioluminescent animals, and conservation suggestions engage visitors in many ways.

For Teachers

Ocean Explorer. oceanexplorer.noaa.gov/forfun/creatures/welcome.html. National
  Oceanic and Atmospheric Administration. (Accessed 4/22/13).
"MySubmarine" incorporates video, audio, fact sheets, and maps from NOAA expeditions into a learning adventure for K-6 students. Expedition education modules and lesson plans help teachers develop ways to use other resources of the website (oceanexplorer.noaa.gov) with students in grades 5-12.

Ocean Portal: Find Your Blue. ocean.si.edu. Smithsonian Institution. (Accessed 4/22/13).
Photos, articles, and video clips provide extensive coverage of topics from ancient seas to contemporary explorations such as the Census of Marine Life. Users can learn about ocean features such as hydrothermal vents or view animals and plants. An educator section includes K-12 lessons and activities.

MEDIA PICKS

Earth Science in Action: Oceans. DVD. 23 min. with tchr's. guide. Library Video
  Co. 2000. $39.95.
Gr 5-8–Two space-adventuring animated aliens narrate the excellent, well-written script, sprinkling their conversation with the right amount of humorous dialogue. Combining live-action footage, animation, and graphics, the program covers the properties of ocean water, the importance of tides, the topography of the ocean

floor, and the life found at different depths. A hands-on experiment investigates the effect of water temperature on ocean currents.

The Living Oceans (Series). 9 DVDs. 20 min. ea. New Dimension Media. 2007. $49 ea. Gr 5-10–Includes: Adaptations to Underwater Nights; Coral Reefs; Marine Predator-Prey Relationships; Sharks: Species and Survival; Starfish Ecological Communities; Symbiosis in Ocean Communities; The Great Whales; Venomous Marine Adaptations; The Ecology of Kelp Forests.

Eds. Note: The full version of "Going Deep" is available online at http://bit.ly/1ausKFO

–FOCUS ON–

SCIENTIFIC EXPLORATION

Quantum Leaps and Bounds

By John Peters

John Peters is a Children's Literature Consultant in New York City.

Like their Common Core counterparts in language arts and mathematics, the recently released Next Generation Science Standards (www.nextgenscience.org) are certain to fuel fresh focus on increasing students' store of basic factual knowledge while helping them acquire useful tools for critical thinking and systematic further learning. This is what science and the scientific method have always been about anyway—with the primary goal, always, of understanding the physical universe and our place in it.

The assortment of recent books surveyed below examines both historical milestones and current research that have illuminated our understanding, with explorations in two opposite (or maybe not so opposite) directions: toward the universe's smallest and most fundamental components and forces, and outward to the stars and beyond. Along with picture books, selected fiction and poetry are tucked into this list to demonstrate less typical but no less valid ways of introducing scientific wonders and concepts. Several of the titles also serve to dispel the notion that science is for nerds; the sometimes provocative biographies of nuclear physicists Ernest Rutherford and Richard Feynman, for instance, profile men whose personalities were every bit as big and powerful as their brains.

REAL STUFF
Primary Ingredients Of The Universe

BAXTER, Roberta. Ernest Rutherford and the Birth of the Atomic Age. (Profiles in Science Series). Morgan Reynolds. 2011. PLB $28.95. ISBN 978-1-599-35171-1. Gr 6-8–Though not well known today, Rutherford was a renowned experimental scientist in his own time. Not only did he make epochal discoveries about radiation and the atom's structure, he also trained much of the generation of theoretical physicists who went on to develop nuclear power and quantum physics. This solid profile, well stocked with photos and leads to further information, offers insight into Rutherford's life and character, as well as his brilliant scientific career.

Berne, Jennifer. On a Beam of Light: A Story of Albert Einstein. illus. by Vladimir Radunsky. Chronicle. 2013. Tr $17.99. ISBN 978-0-811-87235-5; ebook $13.99. ISBN 978-1-452-11309-8. Gr 1-4–Einstein transformed dreams of traveling on a light beam into essential discoveries about the nature of light, gravity, space, and time. In the meditative illustrations, he floats on the page, a solitary thinker pondering the universe's mysteries; more personal images of his "favorite shoes," "favorite equation" (guess!), and "favorite saggy-baggy pants" help to bring him down to Earth (and closer to mortals like us). Closing notes for older readers detail Einstein's insights and later career.

Hawking, Stephen & Lucy Hawking. George and the Big Bang. illus. by Garry Parsons. S & S. 2012. Tr $18.99. ISBN 978-1-442-44005-0; pap. $10.99. ISBN 978-1-4424-4006-7; ebook $9.99. ISBN 978-1-4424-4007-4. Gr 5-7–The third in the Hawkings' occasionally suspenseful and always informative science-fiction adventures sends young George and his friends to the Large Hadron Collider for more near disasters and further exposure to scientific concepts related to the universe's macro and underlying structures. Thanks to a flurry of mini essays by Stephen and other real-life scientists, readers will come away with plenty of brain-stretching quantum and other physics concepts.

Ottaviani, Jim. Feynman. illus. by Leland Myrick. First Second. 2011. Tr $29.99.ISBN 978-1-596-43259-8; pap. $19.99. ISBN 978-1-596-43827-9; ebook $9.99. ISBN 978-1-466-83244-2.

Gr 6 Up–Presented in graphic format, this searching biography offers a multidimensional portrait of a theoretical physicist known as much for his vivid, irreverent character as for his profound insights into how the universe works on the subatomic level. Along with the ups and downs of his personal life, his brilliant, relentless curiosity about the nature of reality will make a lasting impression on readers.

RIGHT STUFF

Astronauts (and Space Probes) at Work

Anderson, Michael. Pioneers in Astronomy and Space Exploration. Rosen. 2012. PLB $32.90. ISBN 978-1-615-30695-4.

Gr 5-7–From Galileo and Isaac Newton to Neil Armstrong and Sally Ride, the 37 historical figures systematically profiled here form a roster of thinkers, observers, and doers who probed the high frontier and went—in one way or another—where none had gone before. These are the giants on whose shoulders the explorers of today can stand.

J
629. 4

Bortz, Alfred B. Seven Wonders of Space Technology. (Seven Wonders Series). 21st Century. 2011. PLB $33.26. ISBN 978-0-761-35453-6.

Gr 4-6–From Stonehenge to the Mars rovers, Bortz charts a select number of technological advances that have played central roles in our understanding of the solar system and the universe beyond. Not only does he present a clear picture of how each "wonder" was constructed and used for new discoveries, he also instills a sense of wonder in readers—particularly in final chapters about future spacecraft and voyages to the stars.

J
629.45

Dell, Pamela. Man on the Moon: How a Photograph Made Anything Seem Possible. (Captured History Series). Compass Point. 2011. PLB $33.99. ISBN 978-0-756-54396-9; pap. $8.99. ISBN 978-0-756-54447-8.

Gr 4-7–Dell relates the eye-opening story of how the electrifying photo of Neil

Armstrong standing on the Moon's surface beneath the Sun's harsh light was made, the immense technological effort that made the photo possible, and how the image came to change people's perceptions of our future in space. A case study in how a picture can be worth much, much more than a thousand words.

Holden, Henry M. The Coolest Job in the Universe: Working Aboard the International Space Station. Enslow. 2012. PLB $23.93. ISBN 978-0-766-04074-8; pap. $7.95. ISBN 978-1-464-40077-3.
Gr 4-6–With an enticing mix of photos and explanatory commentary, this look at life aboard the "Base Camp to the Universe" provides glimpses of the station's residents at work and play. From accounts of how the ISS was built and some of the research that has been done there, readers will come away with new insight into what it will probably be like to live in space, rather than just make short visits.

Rusch, Elizabeth. The Mighty Mars Rovers: The Incredible Adventures of Spirit and Opportunity. (Scientists in the Field Series). Houghton Harcourt. 2012. RTE $18.99. ISBN 978-0-547-47881-4; ebook $18.99. ISBN 978-0-547-82280-8.
Gr 4-6–Rusch takes readers to the red planet, where a 2003 exploratory mission that was initially scheduled to last just 90 (Martian) days is still ongoing. Photos aplenty depict the rugged Martian surface, the scientists back on Earth who planned the mission and nursed it through numerous crises, and the two rovers—down to one now—that survived so long past their expected lifetimes. Mighty, indeed!

Silverman, Buffy. Exploring Dangers in Space: Asteroids, Space Junk, and More. (What's Amazing About Space? Series). Lerner. 2012. PLB $20.95. ISBN 978-0-761-35446-8; pap. $8.95. ISBN 978-0-7613-7882-2.
Gr 2-4–Recent news events (not to mention disaster movies) have raised awareness of the destructive potential of high-speed encounters with both natural and artificial space objects. Not that the hazards haven't always been there—just ask the dinosaurs—but this clearly written and evocatively illustrated introduction gives readers a clearer idea of just what to worry about as well as how scientists search for asteroids or other items on a collision course with our planet.

Sklansky, Amy. Out of This World: Poems and Facts About Space. illus. by Stacey Schuett. Knopf. 2012. Tr $17.99. ISBN 978-0-375-86459-9.
Gr 3-5–"The highest mountain is on Mars,/the deepest canyon too./Yet clouds of

dust could stop me from admiring the view." In poetry laced with fact and supplemented by substantial prose commentary in sidebars, Sklansky presents readers with a space tour that is both informative and vividly experienced. Schuett's dark, starry illustrations add an appropriate sense of depth and distance.

Snedden, Robert. How Do Scientists Explore Space? (Earth, Space, and Beyond Series). Raintree. 2011. PLB $33.99. ISBN 978-1-410-94158-9; pap. $8.99. ISBN 978-1-410-94164-0.
Gr 5-7–Budding astronomers will get a good grounding in the tools of the trade with this basic but broadly focused survey of types of telescopes, kinds of satellites, and some major space probes—and what they all can tell us about the universe. Big, bright photos add revealing visual aids.

Weitekamp, Margaret A. with David DeVorkin. Pluto's Secret: An Icy World's Tale of Discovery. illus. by Diane Kidd. Abrams. 2013. Tr $16.95. ISBN 978-1-419-70423-9.
Gr 2-4–Illustrated with cartoon scenes of Pluto itself literally dancing about in its strange orbit ("Cha-cha/Cha-cha-cha") and making side comments, this lighthearted account of the search for "Planet X" is at once compelling and amusing. Besides giving due notice to one of modern astronomy's greatest discoveries, the informal illustrations and hand-lettered-style narrative add a winning sense of fun.

FAR-OUT STUFF
· · · · · · · · · · · · · · · · · · ·
Wonders of Deep Space

Carson, Mary Kay. Beyond the Solar System: Exploring Galaxies, Black Holes, Alien Planets, and More: A History with 21 Activities. Chicago Review Press. 2013. pap. $18.95. ISBN 978-1-613-74544-1.
Gr 3-6–Enhancing this mind-expanding survey of our historical progress in discovering what the universe is like beyond the atmosphere, low-tech projects made with commonly available materials—from a model of the constellation Orion to a telescope—provide young dreamers and experimenters with hands-on tickets to the stars. The projects and Carson's introductions to the work of astronomers, past and present, are illustrated with a generous mix of photos, diagrams, and line drawings.

Decristofano, Carolyn Cinami. A Black Hole Is Not a Hole. illus. by Michael Carroll. Charlesbridge. 2012. Tr $18.95. ISBN 978-1-570-91783-7.

Gr 4-6–"A black hole is nothing to look at. Literally." With great verve and a rare ability to explain weird physics clearly, DeCristofano introduces young readers to the basics of star life cycles, gravity, how black holes form, and where they are found. The mix of astronomical photographs and artist's conceptions add both insight and drama to this spectacular look at some of nature's most inscrutable and (literally!) attractive phenomena. Audio version available from Live Oak Media.

Hosford, Kate. Infinity and Me. illus. by Gabi Swiatkowska. Carolrhoda. 2012. RTE $16.95. ISBN 978-0-761-36726-0.

Gr 1-4–Looking at the stars raises a question in young Uma's mind, and by sharing that question with others and mulling their various responses, she comes not to comprehend infinity (who could?) but to reach a wise, philosophical accommodation with it. The beautiful illustrations add seemingly paradoxical (but not really) notes of intimacy, and closing comments expand on both the concept and how it is applied in science and mathematics.

Jackson, Ellen. Mysterious Universe: Supernovae, Dark Energy, and Black Holes. (Scientists in the Field Series). Houghton Harcourt. 2008. Tr $18. ISBN 978-0-618-56325-8; pap. $8.99. ISBN 978-0-547-51992-0.

Gr 4-6–Ranging farther afield than any other entry in an exemplary series, this introduction to astronomers who study some of the observable universe's strangest and most powerful phenomena will kindle a sense of wonder in readers. They will be amazed not only by deep space mysteries, but also at how our understanding of their causes and nature is leveraged from seemingly inscrutable clues gathered with incredibly sensitive modern telescopes and other instruments. Also memorable here: the photo of a scientist dressed as a black hole.

Kops, Deborah. Exploring Exoplanets. (What's Amazing About Space? Series). Lerner. 2012. PLB $29.95. ISBN 978-0-761-35444-4; pap. $8.95. ISBN 978-0-7613-7878-5.

Gr 2-4–Some of the most exciting news in astronomy these days is coming from scientists who search for planets orbiting other stars—because the planets are there, and in abundance! This simple account of how those scientists work, the tools they use, and some of the dazzling discoveries they are making is illustrated with tanta-lizing images of what those distant worlds may look like close up.

DIGITAL PICKS

Apps

The Night Sky. iCandi Apps. 2013. Version: 1.9.10. iOS, requires 4.3 or later. $.99. Gr 6 Up–With this app, "showing" a smartphone or tablet any portion of the sky overhead, day or night, brings up a directionally oriented map of stars, planets, and even satellites and larger space junk both above and below the horizon. Includes a manual option for 360 degree browsing, a dimmed mode for night viewing, and (for an additional charge) a database of technical facts and data.

3D Sun. **Dr. Tony Phillips, LLC.** 2012. Version: 4.2. iOS, requires 4.0 or later. Free. Gr 4-7–A great way to keep up with current events on our nearest stellar neighbor, this app centers on a zoomable rotating image of the Sun—based on continually updated satellite images and viewable in a range of wavelengths. Also on (figuratively speaking) tap: a news feed (with an "alerts" option for the disaster-minded), a glossary of technical terms, and a thoroughly stunning video gallery of solar flares and prominences.

Tick Bait's Universe. **Marc Gamble.** 2012. Version: 1.0. iOS, requires 5.0 or later. Free. Gr 5 Up–With a particularly effective use of digital animation, this "powers of ten" journey takes viewers from glimpses of the quarks that compose the atoms that make a dog all the way to the galactic superclusters that are the largest structures so far discovered in our universe. Review questions and accurately detailed but infor-mally drawn illustrations add further appeal.

Websites

Amazing Space. amazing-space.stsci.edu. Space Telescope Science Institute. (Ac-cessed 5/21/13).
Gr 5-9–This site offers not only an immense array of photos taken with the Hubble Space Telescope (and a special feature on the HST's 2009 servicing mission), but also many links to other space photo galleries, homework help resources, and a month-by-month guide to the night sky for stargazers.

NASA's Space Place. spaceplace.nasa.gov. National Aeronautics and Space Admin-istration. (Accessed 5/21/13).
Gr 3-6–Lively graphics on the opening page invite young explorers to plunge into

a vast gathering of space pictures and videos, interviews with space scientists, experiments, projects, games, quizzes, and more.

Planet Quest: The Search for Another Earth. planetquest.jpl.nasa.gov. Jet Propulsion Laboratory. California Institute of Technology. NASA. (Accessed 5/21/13). Gr 4 Up–Along with news, NASA's official site for tracking the search for planets in other solar systems offers information about current missions, plenty of photographs, and a planet counter. A gathering of interactive activities allows budding astronomers to create their own planets, plan an interstellar voyage, and even explore "alien" life forms here on Earth.

Sky-Map.org. sky-map.org. Thornhill, Ontario, Canada. (Accessed 5/21/13). Gr 5 Up–Why wait for the sun to go down to explore the night sky? This URL opens a fully detailed, zoomable, searchable star map of the observable universe beyond the solar system, with informational labels, galleries of space photos and art, and even space news.

Eds. Note: The full version of "Quantum Leaps and Bounds"
is available online at http://bit.ly/13SzF9O

Sports

J
796.39

Cook, Sally and Charlton, James. Hey Batta Batta Swing!: The Wild Old Days of Baseball. 48 pp. McElderry (Simon & Schuster Children's Publishing) 2007. ISBN 978-1-4169-1207-1. Illustrated by Ross MacDonald. Baseball's days of yore receive a sunny treatment. Cook and Charlton's chatty text reveals enough tidbits to make the most fanatical fan happy. The narrative is peppered with baseball slang, helpfully glossed in the margins. MacDonald's nostalgic style is a crackerjack match of illustration to text; his predominantly yellow palette lends the whole a happily idealistic feel.
Sports; Sports–Baseball

Crowe, Ellie. Surfer of the Century: The Life of Duke Kahanamoku. 48 pp. Lee 2007. ISBN 978-1-58430-276-6. Illustrated by Richard Waldrep.
Crowe's respectful picture book biography brings to light a seminal figure in the history of surfing and Olympic swimming. She chooses not to make racism the focus of Duke's story but shows through understatement the emotional impact discrimination had on the native Hawaiian swimmer. Waldrep's paintings convey both dignity and dynamism, with ocean scenes hurtling from pages awash in sunlight. Timeline.
Sports; Hawaii; SportsSurfing; Sports–Swimming; Biographies; Kahanamoku, Duke; Prejudices

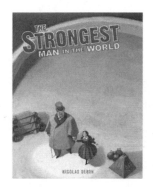

Debon, Nicolas. The Strongest Man in the World: Louis Cyr. 32 pp. Groundwood (House of Anansi Press) 2007. ISBN 978-0-88899-731-9.
At the end of the nineteenth century, Louis Cyr was widely regarded as the world's strongest man. Debon uses the book's graphic novel–style format to communicate immediacy and intimacy, as Cyr relates his life story to his daughter. The close-to-monochromatic palette dominated by warm earth tones is surprisingly pleasing to the eye. An afterword is illustrated with photographs. Bib.
Individual Biographies; Sports–Weight lifting; Cyr, Louis; Québec (Canada); Circuses; Cartoons and comics; Family–Father and daughter; Canada

Nelson, Kadir. We Are the Ship: The Story of Negro League Baseball. 88 pp. Hyperion/Jump (Hyperion Books for Children) 2008. ISBN 978-0-7868-0832-8.
Imagine listening to Willie Mays and Ernie Banks swapping tales. That easygoing, conversational storytelling is what Nelson achieves in this pitch-perfect history of Negro League baseball. His extensive research yields loads of attention-grabbing details. The grand slam, though, is the art: Nelson's oil paintings have a steely dignity, and his from-the-ground perspectives make the players look larger than life. Bib., ind.
Sports; Sports–Baseball; Negro League baseball; African Americans

Smith, Charles R., Jr. Black Jack: The Ballad of Jack Johnson. 40 pp. Roaring Brook/Porter 2010. ISBN 978-1-59643-473-8. Illustrated by Shane W. Evans.
Smith tells the heavyweight champ's story in ballad form, which suits the larger-than-life feel of this dramatic tale. Johnson's quest to be champion was hampered by white title-holders; his persistence was eventually rewarded. The poetry is interspersed with quotes of the time. Evans uses oil paint and ink to depict the deter-

mined fighter, with newspapers, maps, and crowds in the backgrounds. Bib.
Sports; Sports–Boxing; Biographies; African Americans; Johnson, Jack; Poetry

Smith, Charles R., Jr. Twelve Rounds to Glory: The Story of Muhammad Ali. 80 pp. Candlewick 2007. ISBN 978-0-7636-1692-2. Illustrated by Bryan Collier.
This book provides insight into the nuances of Ali's personality and the racism he fought with words and fists. Smith's extensive rhyming text mimics the cadence of the boxer's own poetic bravado; oversize quotes are interspersed. Collier's glowing, dignified mixed-media art captures the intensity of Ali's facial expressions and the explosive athleticism of the fighters. Timeline.
Sports; African Americans; Biographies; Sports–Boxing; Ali, Muhammad; Race relations; Poetry; Prejudices

U.S. History

Anderson, Laurie Halse. Independent Dames: What You Never Knew About the Women and Girls of the American Revolution. 40 pp. Simon (Simon & Schuster Children's Publishing) 2008. ISBN 978-0-689-85808-6. Illustrated by Matt Faulkner.
Anderson's saucy text challenges conventionally taught American Revolutionary history. Readers will be hooked by her thoroughly infectious humor as they learn about the girls and women who organized boycotts, spied on Redcoats, and disguised themselves as male soldiers. Faulkner's detailed ink and watercolor art shows women crashing the scene, while brief paragraphs explain their heroic feats. Reading list, timeline, websites. Bib., ind.
Collective Biographies; History, American–Revolutionary War; Women–History; Gender roles; Women–Biographies

Brown, Don. Gold! Gold from the American River! 64 pp. Roaring Brook/Flash Point 2011. ISBN 978-1-59643-223-9 PE ISBN 978-1-59643-700-5.
Actual Times series. Brown turns his earthy palette and voice to the California Gold Rush. His unique tone is both larger-than-life and precisely detailed, and the treatment suits his subject. Well-composed watercolors convey action and emotion, giving just enough detail and variety. Combining pathos and humor, the book commu-

nicates much with an engaging and brief text, making it a first-choice introduction to the subject. Websites. Bib.

Brown, Don. Henry and the Cannons: An Extraordinary True Story of the American Revolution. 32 pp. Roaring Brook 2013. ISBN 978-1-59643-266-6.
In this followup to *Let It Begin Here!*, stylized watercolors heighten the drama and occasional humor of Henry Knox's mission to bring heavy cannon from Lake Champlain forts to Washington's forces in 1776 Boston. The text hews closely to the record—except for one fact: Brown states, "Washington ached for cannon...But Washington had none," an unfortunate exaggeration of an otherwise "true story." Bib.
North America; Knox, Henry; History, American–Revolutionary War; Massachusetts; History, American–Colonial life; Soldiers

Byrd, Robert. Electric Ben: The Amazing Life and Times of Benjamin Franklin. 40 pp. Dial 2012. ISBN 978-0-8037-3749-5.

Byrd divides Franklin's life into seventeen whimsically labeled double-page spreads covering topics ranging from his fascination with electricity to his ideas for social progress to his diplomatic roles. Informative, exploratory, nonpandering text is set on attractive pages; spot art and larger illustrations provide information and present a visual record. This book shimmers with excitement, begging to be read. Reading list, timeline. Bib.
Individual Biographies; Inventions and inventors; Statesmen; Franklin, Benjamin; Scientists; History, American–Revolutionary War; Electricity; Diplomats; Printing

Colman, Penny. Thanksgiving: The True Story. 149 pp. Holt/Ottaviano 2008. ISBN 978-0-8050-8229-6.
This investigation into Thanksgiving's roots covers many topics, from Sarah Josepha Hale's quest to make it a national holiday to the origins of Thanksgiving football games. Colman's strength is sharing her research process with readers, starting with a survey designed to elicit questions about the holiday, and indicating the ways those responses led her to her own search for further information. Timeline. Bib., ind.
Customs and Holidays; Holidays–Thanksgiving; Native Americans–North America; History, American–Colonial life

Denenberg, Barry. Lincoln Shot: A President's Life Remembered. 40 pp. Feiwel (Holtz-brinck Publishers) 2008. ISBN 978-0-312-37013-8 PE ISBN 978-0-312-60442-4. Illustrated by Christopher Bing.

Denenberg and Bing create an invented newspaper memorial of Lincoln's death, with yellowed pages bound in faux-weathered maroon. Archival photographs and maps, as well as artificial advertisements (e.g., fountain pen nibs), appear alongside portraits that mimic period engravings. Beautifully integrating content and form, this engrossing oversized (twelve by eighteen inches) book serves both browsers and researchers well. Timeline. Ind.

Individual Biographies; History, American–Civil War; Newspapers; Journalism; Presidents–United States; Lincoln, Abraham

○ **Ferris, Jeri Chase.** Noah Webster & His Words. Houghton (Houghton Mifflin Trade and Reference Division) 2012. ISBN 978-0-547-39055-0. Illustrated by Vincent X. Kirsch.

In this unique biography of the patriot and dictionary writer, Ferris seamlessly incorporates words with their definitions—"He wanted to write a DIC-TION-AR-Y (noun: a book listing words in ABC order, telling what they mean and how to spell them)"—creating opportunities for vocabulary development, but also showing what Webster's work was all about. Kirsch's humorous illustrations highlight important moments. Timeline, websites. Bib.

Individual Biographies; Teachers; Dictionaries; Language–Vocabulary; Webster, Noah; History, American–Revolutionary War; Books and reading

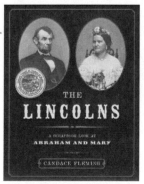

Fleming, Candace. The Lincolns: A Scrapbook Look at Abraham and Mary. 181 pp. Random/Schwartz & Wade 2008. ISBN 978-0-375-83618-3 LE ISBN 978-0-375-93618-0. (Also Nonfic 973.7092 F)

This book is chock-full of reproductions of primary sources, both textual and visual, and an abundance of interesting anecdotes. It's equally inviting for reference, browsing, or pleasure reading. Moreover, by giving Mary's story equal weight, Fleming gives us not only greater insight into each of them but also a fuller picture of their world. Reading list, timeline, websites. Ind.

Individual Biographies; Lincoln, Abraham; Lincoln, Mary Todd; History, American–Colonial life; Presidents–United States; Presidents' spouses; First ladies; Women–Presidents' spouses

Foster, Mark. Whale Port. 64 pp. Houghton/Lorraine 2007. ISBN 978-0-618-54722-7. Illustrated by Gerald Foster.

Readers follow development of the imagined whaling town of Tuckanucket. We see industries grow: shipsmithing, candleworks, milling—and, later, tourism. Each precisely detailed ink and crayon double-page spread is drawn from the same bird's-eye perspective, allowing readers to spot landmarks and changes; additional interspersed pages offer elaboration. The Fosters have elegantly synthesized a tremendous amount of information into a beguiling format. Ind.

North America; Whaling; Animals–Whales; New England; History, American–Colonial life; City and town life

⊝ **Freedman, Russell.** Lafayette and the American Revolution. 88 pp. Holiday 2010. ISBN 978-0-8234-2182-4.

Lafayette, a nobleman in the French court, risked everything to aid the American cause of liberty. He also played a prominent role in the French Revolution and had a long career in French politics. The narrative, written with all of Freedman's characteristic grace and clarity, presents in Lafayette an outsider's perspective on the American Revolution. Illustrated with artwork reproductions. Timeline. Bib., ind.

Individual Biographies; Lafayette, Marie Joseph Paul Yves Roch Gilbert Du Motier, marquis de; History, American–Revolutionary War; Generals; Statesmen; France; French Revolution

J
973.3 **Freedman, Russell.** Washington at Valley Forge. 100 pp. Holiday 2008. ISBN 978-0-8234-2069-8.

Freedman again illuminates a piece of American history: here, the Revolutionary War, using the winter of 1777–78 as a focal point. His customary graceful prose, eye for the telling detail, and clear narrative arc make this a pleasure to read. Frequent quotations, including first-person reminiscences, and judiciously chosen artistic interpretations add to the appeal of this invitingly designed book. Maps, source notes, timeline. Bib., ind.

North America; History, American–Revolutionary War; Valley Forge (PA); Washington, George; Pennsylvania

J
811 **Grady, Cynthia.** I Lay My Stitches Down: Poems of American Slavery. 40 pp. Eerdmans 2011. ISBN 978-0-8028-5386-8. Illustrated by Michele Wood.

Grady crafts her fourteen poems to honor the art of quiltmaking. Pieces recall quilt squares by using ten lines of ten syllables each. Working in intensely hued acrylics, Wood bases her quilt-shaped designs on the patterns that give the poems their titles, incorporating forms into carefully composed scenes inhabited by heroic, emo-

tion-charged figures. Author's and illustrator's notes are appended. Reading list.
Poetry; Slavery; African Americans; Quilts

○ **Hoose, Phillip.** Claudette Colvin: Twice Toward Justice. 133 pp. Farrar/Kroupa 2009.
ISBN 978-0-374-31322-7 PE ISBN 978-0-312-66105-2.
In 1955 Montgomery, Alabama, fifteen-year-old Colvin refused to give up her seat on
the bus. Hoose fashions a compelling narrative that balances the momentous events
of the civil rights movement with the personal crises of a courageous young woman. This vivid and dramatic account, complemented with photographs, sidebars, and
liberal excerpts from interviews with Colvin, reasserts her place in history. Bib., ind.
*Individual Biographies; Colvin, Claudette; Civil rights; Race relations; Women–African Americans;
African Americans; Montgomery (AL); Women–Civil rights; Women–Biographies; Prejudices*

King, Martin Luther, Jr. I Have a Dream. 32 pp. Ran-
dom/Schwartz & Wade 2012. ISBN 978-0-
375-85887-1 LE ISBN 978-0-375-95887-8.
Illustrated by Kadir Nelson.
In superlative oil paintings, Nelson brings to life this
famous speech. He begins with Dr. King at the Lincoln Memorial addressing the crowd; literal illustrations of his words (e.g., his "four little children")
follow. Visually, this is a stunning accomplishment
that embodies the thrilling inspiration of Dr. King's
words. The complete text of the speech is appended; accompanying CD included.
*Government/Economics/and Education; History, American; African Americans; Civil
rights; King, Martin Luther, Jr.; Washington (DC); Clergy*

◎ **Nelson, Scott Reynolds.** Ain't Nothing but a Man: My Quest to Find the Real John Henry.
64 pp. National (National Geographic Books) 2008. ISBN 978-1-4263-0000-
4 LE ISBN 978-1-4263-0001-1.
With Marc Aronson. Nelson follows clues, from song lyrics to census data, engineering reports, and prison records, tracking a folk hero who originated in the reality of
1870s racial injustice. Sepia historical photographs on buff paper, with scarlet captions
and occasional overlays, depict the setting and cast for this gripping, meticulously
documented saga. Reading list, websites. Ind.
*North America; Songs–Folk songs; Vehicles–Trains; African Americans; Railroads; Race re-
lations; Folklore–African American*

Nelson, Vaunda Micheaux. Bad News for Outlaws: The Remarkable Life of Bass Reeves, Deputy U.S. Marshal. 40 pp. Carolrhoda 2009. ISBN 978-0-8225-6764-6. Illustrated by R. Gregory Christie.

Bass Reeves, born a slave, captured over three thousand outlaws as a deputy U.S. marshal. This captivating biography is told in language as colorful as Reeves's career. Accentuated with a palette knife, Christie's sharply textured paintings create an impressionist background of an unformed land as well as detailed portraits of Reeves, his bold black hat conveying unmistakable authority. Reading list, timeline, websites. Bib., ind.

Individual Biographies; African Americans; History, American–Frontier and pioneer life; West (U.S.); Robbers and outlaws; Reeves, Bass

J Our White House: Looking In, Looking Out. 242 pp. Candlewick 2008. ISBN 978-0-975. 3 7636-2067-7 PE ISBN 978-0-7636-4609-7.

From Natalie Babbitt and Jon Scieszka to R. Gregory Christie and Steven Kellogg, 108 writers and artists take readers on a virtual tour of 1600 Pennsylvania Avenue. The voices and images, roughly chronological, recognize those living inside and others observing from the outside. Unique bits and pieces create a browser's dream as readers explore the nooks and crannies of American history. Sources. Ind.

North America; White House; Politics; Washington (DC); Presidents–United States; History, American; Government

◯ **Partridge, Elizabeth.** Marching for Freedom: Walk Together, Children, and Don't You Grow Weary. 72 pp. Viking 2009. ISBN 978-0-670-01189-6.

Partridge writes about the civil rights march from Selma to Montgomery from the viewpoint of children and teenagers who participated. Their recollections, culled largely from author interviews, perfectly balance and complement the information about the adults—Martin Luther King, George Wallace, Lyndon Johnson—that typically dominate historical accounts. The accompanying archival photographs have a moral impact as well as a visual one. Bib., ind.

Government/Economics/and Education; Voting; African Americans; Race relations; Civil rights; Alabama; Children

◯ **Ray, Deborah Kogan.** Down the Colorado: John Wesley Powell, the One-Armed Explorer. 48 pp. Farrar/Foster 2007. ISBN 978-0-374-31838-3.

In 1869 Powell led the first recorded expedition down the Green and Colorado rivers, mapping the Grand Canyon. Ray emphasizes Powell's accomplishments in text and art: primarily full-page illustrations, spacious watercolors in natural colors of the

West. The book's pacing allows readers, like Powell, to experience the natural beauty around them. A helpful map and author's note complete the book. Timeline. Bib.
Individual Biographies; Disabilities, Physical; Exploration and explorers; Colorado River; Rivers; History, American–Frontier and pioneer life; Powell, John Wesley; West (U.S.); Grand Canyon (AZ); Maps

◯ **Sheinkin, Steve.** King George: What Was His Problem?: Everything Your Schoolbooks Didn't Tell You About the American Revolution. 195 pp. Roaring Brook/Flash Point 2008. ISBN 978-1-59643-319-9 PE ISBN 978-1-59643-518-6. Illustrated by Tim Robinson.
Sheinkin's entertaining histories cover the Revolutionary and Civil wars. *George* (originally *Storyteller's History: The American Revolution*) begins with thirteen ways to start a revolution. *Miserable* opens with thirteen ways to rip a country apart. Each book includes personal, frequently irreverent, accounts of the participants. The layouts invite browsing: bold subheadings, short exposition, numerous pen-and-ink cartoonlike illustrations, and plenty of maps. Bib., ind. Review covers these titles: *King George: What Was His Problem?* and *Two Miserable Presidents*.
North America; History, American–Revolutionary War; History, American–Colonial life; George III, King of Great Britain

◯ **Sheinkin, Steve.** Two Miserable Presidents: Everything Your Schoolbooks Didn't Tell You About the Civil War. 220 pp. Roaring Brook/Flash Point 2008. ISBN 978-1-59643-320-5 PE ISBN 978-1-59643-519-3. Illustrated by Tim Robinson.
Sheinkin's entertaining histories cover the Revolutionary and Civil wars. *George* (originally *Storyteller's History: The American Revolution*) begins with thirteen ways to start a revolution. *Miserable* opens with thirteen ways to rip a country apart. Each book includes personal, frequently irreverent, accounts of the participants. The layouts invite browsing: bold subheadings, short exposition, numerous pen-and-ink cartoonlike illustrations, and plenty of maps. Bib., ind. Review covers these titles: *King George: What Was His Problem?* and *Two Miserable Presidents*.
North America; Presidents–United States; History, American–Colonial life; History, American–Civil War; Presidents–Confederate States of America; Lincoln, Abraham; Davis, Jefferson

J **Silvey, Anita.** I'll Pass for Your Comrade: Women Soldiers in the Civil War. 118 pp. Clar-
973.7 ion 2008. ISBN 978-0-618-57491-9. Also Y973.708
Why did women, disguised as men, fight in the Civil War? How did they pass? And how did these remarkable women transition back into civilian life? Silvey builds an

engaging social history around these questions, interspersing solid factual exposition with colorful vignettes and period illustrations and photographs. The broader contexts of the war and the mores of the time give additional resonance. Bib., ind.

North America; Gender roles; History, American–Civil War; Women–Biographies; Soldiers; Women–History; Biographies

○ **Wadsworth, Ginger.** First Girl Scout: The Life of Juliette Gordon Low. 210 pp. Clarion 2011. ISBN 978-0-547-24394-8.

In 1912, Low founded the Girl Scouts—a pioneering organization designed to help empower girls of all races and ethnicities. Information is provided about the organization (e.g., origins of cookie-selling) and its continued success after Low's death in 1927. Wadsworth captures Low's stubborn but charismatic spirit by blending facts and humorous sketches in this winning biography. Numerous archival photos supplement the text. Reading list, timeline, websites. Bib., ind.

Individual Biographies; Low, Juliette Gordon; Women–Biographies; Scouts and scouting; Girl Scouts; Disabilities, Physical–Deafness

· ·

—FOCUS ON—
Westward Expansion

California Bound

By Mary Mueller

*Mary Mueller, a retired librarian, is now a substitute teacher
and librarian for the Rolla Public Schools in Rolla, MO.*

· ·

From a European perspective, North America's Western coast was one of the most remote places on Earth, yet its location and perceived riches would make it a focus of at least four countries' expansionist designs. It bordered the "Spanish Lake" of the Pacific, but Spain paid it scant attention, concentrating instead on Mexico's mineral riches and lucrative Manila trade. Other European powers quickly recognized opportunities for empire and trade. Russia viewed Alaska and the Pacific Northwest as an extension of its vast nation and a valuable source of furs. England saw supply ports for its growing empire and commercial opportunity in the region. British and Russian incursions along the coast provoked Spain, which established a string of missions in California as a buffer for its Mexican holdings, but was unable to prevent Russian and British claims farther north. However, sailing distances from Europe remained so daunting that the region's development was desultory at best.

It would be the Americans who changed the dynamic in the Pacific West. After the Revolutionary War, American seamen developed a thriving China and whaling trade. Those traders saw the region's deep ports and natural resources as ripe for American "enterprise." A growing stream of Americans, confident and unshakable in their "Manifest Destiny" to rule the entire continent, flowed into California and the Oregon Territory, displacing indigenous Native Americans and settlers from several nations. Oregon's boundaries were settled by diplomacy, and the Mexican War provided the pretext for John Frémont to seize California without firing a shot.

Although the region became part of the United States, its diverse culture and heritage were heavily influenced by its international past, and this unique culture and history are certain to resonate with students.

ELEMENTARY SCHOOL

Bergin, Mark. You Wouldn't Want to Travel with Captain Cook!: A Voyage You'd Rather Not Make. 2006. ISBN 978-1-439-52364-3; ISBN 978-0-531-12446-8.

Stewart, David. You Wouldn't Want to Explore with Sir Francis Drake: A Pirate You'd Rather Not Know. 2005. ISBN 978-1-439-52363-6; ISBN 978-0-531-12393-5. ea. vol: illus. by David Antram. Scholastic. PLB $18.95; pap. $9.95.

Gr 3-5–Based on the accounts of men who sailed with Cook and Drake, these books combine limited text with captioned, caricature-style cartoons to provide a lighthearted but realistic look at the exploits and achievements of the expeditions and the perils of shipboard life. Gross and gruesome details will attract and hold readers' attention.

Bial, Raymond. Missions and Presidios. (American Community Series). Children's Press. 2004. PLB $29. ISBN 978-1-417-65015-6.

Gr 3-5–Bial introduces readers to the vast Spanish colonial presence in early America, describing how missions and presidios in Florida, Texas, New Mexico, Arizona, and California served the empire's dual goals of conquest and Christianization and left an enduring cultural legacy, particularly in the Southwestern United States.

Domnauer, Teresa. Westward Expansion. (A True Bk.) Children's Press. 2010. PLB $26. ISBN 978-0-531-20586-0.

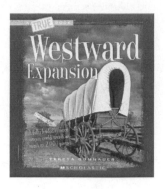

Gr 3-5–Domnauer covers the entire American frontier period in this introduction, focusing on the diversity of the groups and individuals who ventured across the continent and the changes they brought to Native peoples. Large, captioned illustrations, interesting factoids, and a "True Statistics" summary page are included.

Gendell, Megan. The Spanish Missions of California. (A True Bk.). Children's Press. 2010. PLB $28. ISBN 978-0-531-20580-8; pap. $6.95. 978-0-531-21243-1.

Gr 3-5–With an appealing and readable layout and colorful, captioned photographs and maps, this introductory overview describes why and how these missions were established, their patterns of work and worship, and their devastating effects on Indian culture. Readers also learn about surviving missions and how they influenced California culture and agriculture.

Parker, Lewis K. John Jacob Astor and the Fur Trade. (Reading Power Series). Rosen/PowerKids Press. 2003. PLB $21.25. ISBN 978-0-823-96447-5.

Gr 3-6–Astor was among the first to recognize the potential of the Pacific fur trade, and his fur profits became the foundation of a vast fortune. Simple biographical information is presented in an attractive format that includes large print, high-quality period illustrations, contemporary photos, and maps.

Sonneborn, Liz. The Chumash. (Native American Histories Series). Lerner. 2007. PLB $27.93. ISBN 978-0-822-55912-2; pap. $8.95. ISBN 978-0-822-55912-2.

Gr 3-6–The Chumash tribe thrived on the Pacific's bounty in California's mild climate, but its people were decimated by European diseases and forced labor in Spanish missions. Sonneborn describes the origins, traditions, and culture of the Chumash, who still survive and are enjoying a contemporary renaissance.

Yin. Coolies. illus. by Chris Soentpiet. Philomel. 2001. RTE $17.99. ISBN 978-0-399-23227-5; pap. $7.99. ISBN 978-0-142-50055-2.

Gr 3-5–Leaving China to support their family, Shek and his younger brother travel to America, where they work building the transcontinental railroad. Known as coolies, they endure backbreaking labor, discrimination, and danger but never lose faith in one another or the promise of a better life. Arresting illustrations capture the scope and drama of the siblings' adventures.

MIDDLE GRADE FICTION

Fleischman, Sid. The Giant Rat of Sumatra or Pirates Galore. Greenwillow. 2005. PLB $14.99. ISBN 978-1-435-25276-9; pap. $6.99. ISBN 978-0-060-74240-9.

Gr 4-8–Twelve-year-old Edmond "Shipwreck" Peters, rescued at sea by a pirate vessel, navigates the dangers of San Diego during the Mexican War and resolves the conflict between loyalty to his Mexican rescuer and homesickness for Boston. This charming coming-of-age story blends adventure, mystery, and humor.

Garland, Sherry. Valley of the Moon: The Diary of María Rosalia de Milagros, Sonoma Valley, Alta California, 1846. (Dear America Series). Scholastic. 2001. Tr $10.95. ISBN 978-0-439-08820-6.

Gr 5-8–Rosa, an orphaned mestizo servant, records her work and the rhythms of life in a California rancho, the search for her own family roots, and the growing turmoil caused by the Americans who are pouring into California to overthrow Mexican rule and claim the land.

O'Dell, Scott. Island of the Blue Dolphins. 1960. Tr $16. ISBN 978-0-395-06962-2; pap. $6.99. ISBN 978-0-547-32861-4.

——. Zia. 1995. pap. $6.99. ISBN 978-0-547-40633-6. ea vol: Houghton.

Gr 5-8–Karana, a California Indian girl, is left behind when her tribe abandons its island home after a devastating battle with Aleuts who hunt furs for the Russians. Living alone for 18 years, she maintains her traditional ways, but her rescue brings her into the changed world of the Spanish missions. In *Zia*, Karana's niece leaves a Spanish mission to rescue her aunt. Both struggle with the restrictions and constraints of mission life.

MIDDLE GRADE NONFICTION

Aronson, Marc & John W. Glenn. The World Made New: Why the Age of Exploration Happened and How It Changed the World. National Geographic. 2007. Tr $17.95. ISBN 978-0-792-26454-5; PLB $27.90. ISBN 978-0-792-26978-6.

Gr 5-8–The authors explain how the age of European exploration ushered in the modern era of mobility, trade and exchange, and scientific advances while leaving a tragic legacy of decimating disease and the colonial domination of indigenous peoples. Large, attractive period illustrations and maps supplement the text.

Aykroyd, Clarissa. Exploration of the California Coast: The Adventures of Juan Rodríguez Cabrillo, Francis Drake, Sebastián Vazcaíno, and Other Explorers of North America's West Coast. (Exploration and Discovery Series). Mason Crest. 2003. PLB $19.95. ISBN 978-1-590-84043-6.
Gr 4-7–The remote California frontier became an international conflict point when British vessels began to explore and lay claim to regions under Spanish control. Aykroyd profiles the explorers, discusses their voyages, and explains how they affected the international balance of power and triggered Spanish colonization of California.

Crompton, Samuel Willard. Francis Drake and the Oceans of the World. (Explorers of New Worlds Series). Chelsea House. 2006. PLB $30. ISBN 978-0-791-08615-5.
Gr 5-8–Crompton places Drake's life and voyages into the context of British-Spanish enmity during the Age of Exploration, when his piracy terrorized Spanish settlements and his probes of Spanish possessions in the Pacific Northwest provoked Spanish action. Students looking for substantial report material will find it here.

Currie, Stephen. Thar She Blows: American Whaling in the Nineteenth Century. (People's History Series). Lerner. 2001. PLB $26.60. ISBN 978-0-822-50646-1.
Gr 6 Up–Currie objectively examines the lives of the "First American Tourists" who roved the globe on whalers, describing the thrill and danger of chasing and killing these animals, the difficult and poorly paid onboard work, the toll that whaling took on sailors and their families, and the end of the whaling era. Black-and-white photographs add interest.

Doak, Robin. Voices from Colonial America: California, 1542-1850. National Geographic. 2006. Tr $21.95. ISBN 978-0-792-26391-3; PLB $ 32.90. ISBN 978-0-792-26861-1.
Gr 5-8–Primary-source excerpts and period illustrations augment this account of early California. The author describes how international interest in the region pushed Spanish settlement, details the lives of the Europeans and indigenous peoples during the Spanish and Mexican periods, and explains how the American takeover and discovery of gold changed California's culture, population, and economy.

○ **Faber, Harold.** John Charles Frémont: Pathfinder to the West. (Great Explorations Series). Marshall Cavendish. 2003. PLB $32.79. ISBN 978-0-761-41481-0.
Gr 6-8–The impetuous Frémont, acting under secret orders from President Polk, seized Mexican California and its riches for the United States at the outbreak of the Mexican War without firing a shot. Faber examines the explorer's outsized life and feats and his significance in American expansion into the Pacific West.

J
9 2 **Harness, Cheryl.** The Tragic Tale of Narcissa Whitman and a Faithful History of the Oregon Trail. illus. by author. National Geographic. 2006. Tr $16.95. ISBN 978-0-792-25920-6.

Gr 5-8–Missionary Narcissa Whitman was one of the first American women to journey to Oregon. Her story is interwoven with background about American exploration, the Northwest fur trade, and the burgeoning American settlement that brought the Oregon Territory into the United States. Varied black-and-white illustrations include maps, time lines, and drawings.

○ **Isserman, Maurice.** Exploring North America 1800-1900. ISBN 978-1-604-13194-9.
——. **Vail, Martha.** Exploring the Pacific. ISBN 978-1-604-13197-0.
ea. vol: rev. ed. (Discovery and Exploration Series.) Chelsea House. 2010. PLB $35.
Gr 6-8–The first book summarizes the commercial and expansionist goals that were the driving force for Jefferson's "other explorers," the fur traders of the northwest; John C. Frémont's annexation of California; and the American influx into Alaska. The author also analyzes how exploration contributed to scientific and geographical knowledge and encouraged the conservationist movement. Vail traces the paths of Pacific explorers from early indigenous inhabitants to imperialistic Europeans to brash Americans in search of commerce and empire, who, in doing so, developed and employed advances in scientific knowledge and technology.

○ **Keremitsis, Eileen.** Life in a California Mission. (The Way People Live Series). Lucent. 2003. PLB $30.85. ISBN 978-1-590-18159-1.
Gr 5-8–The lasting cultural and agricultural importance of Spanish missions is conveyed in this objective overview that details the daily lives of the friars, officials, and baptized Indians who labored there and discusses the rapid decline of the missions when the newly independent Mexico awarded the mission land to settlers.

○ **Lilly, Alexandra.** Spanish Colonies in America. (We the People Series). Compass Point. 2009. PLB $27.99. ISBN 978-0-756-53840-8.

Gr 4-6–Interspersed with full-color paintings, maps, and photographs, this clear summary follows Spanish explorers whose search for riches laid claim to vast regions for Spain and the missions and outposts they established. The empire's disastrous effect on indigenous peoples and the enduring Spanish contributions to the American economy and culture are also considered.

○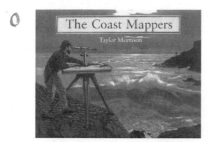

Morrison, Taylor. The Coast Mappers. Houghton. 2004. Tr $17. ISBN 978-0-618-25408-8.

Gr 5-8–In 1850, the U.S. Coast Survey sent George Davidson to chart America's Pacific Coast. This attractive account, which includes many of Davidson's original drawings, describes how his surveyors overcame enormous challenges to create maps that opened the region to international trade and gives readers a unique perspective on the region's maritime history.

○ **Murphy, Jim.** Gone A-Whaling: The Lure of the Sea and the Hunt for the Great Whale. Clarion. 1998. Tr $18. ISBN 978-0-395-69847-1; ebook $8.95. ISBN 978-0-547-34630-4.

Gr 6-9–Excerpts from primary sources enhance this detailed examination of whaling from prehistory to the present. Murphy focuses on the practices and excesses of its 18th- and 19th-century heyday, while period illustrations and sidebar descriptions of whale species help readers better understand life on whaling ships and its environmental consequences.

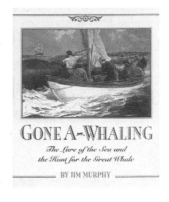

○ **Van Meter, Larry.** Yerba Buena. (Colonial Settlements in America Series). Chelsea House. 2007. PLB $30. ISBN 978-0-791-09338-2.

Gr 6-10–Early European explorers sailed past the narrow entrance to San Francisco's immense harbor, but when the Spanish discovered the port they named Yerba Buena, it quickly became an important trade center as well as a strategic buffer against British and Russian encroachment. Van Meter's history pays particular attention to the damaging impact on the indigenous population.

Q **Williams, Jack S. & Thomas L. Davis.** Craftsmen and Craftswomen of the California Mission Frontier. ISBN 978-0-823-96280-8.

———. Indians of the California Mission Frontier.ISBN 978-0-823-96281-5.

———. Padres of the California Mission Frontier. ISBN 978-0-8239-6283-9.

———. Sailors, Merchants, and Muleteers of the California Mission Frontier. ISBN 978-0-823-96282-2.

———. Soldiers and Their Families of the California Mission Frontier. ISBN 978-0-823-96285-3.

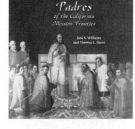

———. Townspeople and Ranchers of the California Mission Frontier. ISBN 978-0-823-96284-6.

ea vol: (People of the California Missions Series). Rosen. 2004. PLB $29.25.

Gr 4-8–Clear writing, ample background information, and an attractive format that features period art, maps, and contemporary photos distinguish these detailed examinations of the groups living in California during the mission and rancho periods, giving readers valuable insight on how this critical period influenced the development and culture of the region.

ON THE WEB

For Students

"California as I Saw It": First-Person Narratives of California's Early Years, 1849-1900. lcweb2.1oc.gov/ammem/cbhtml/cbhome.html. American Memory Collection. Library of Congress. (Accessed 12/9/13).

Gr 5 Up–This collection of readings and period illustrations includes the section "Early California History: An Overview," which provides well-written and objective background about the geography, people, and political and religious organization of the region before it came under American control.

California History Online. californiahistoricalsociety.org/timeline/main.html. California Historical Society. (Accessed 12/9/13).

Gr 5 Up–This site's easy-to-use interactive time line features brief main and subtopic essays by historian James J. Rawls about the diverse groups and nations that influenced the region as well as period illustrations from the society's collection.

California Missions Resource Center. www.missionscalifornia.com. Pentacle Press. (Accessed 12/9/13).

Gr 5 Up–Although this site does sell publisher products, the mission histories are supplemented with detailed information about individual settlements and an inter-active "Ask the Experts" section. User friendly and informative.

Columbia River History Project. www.ccrh.org/center/projects.php. Northwest Power
and Conservation Council. (Accessed 12/9/13).
Gr 8 Up–Although lacking in visual appeal, the entries on this site provide encyclo-pedic coverage of the environmental, social, and economic history of the Columbia
River Basin region, including exploration, international competition and conflict,
fur trade, missionaries, and indigenous peoples.

For Teachers

Age of Exploration. marinersmuseum.org/education/age-exploration. The Mariners'
Museum. Newport News, VA. (Accessed 12/2/13).
A large collection of readings, lesson plans, activities, period maps, and illustrations
about the Age of Exploration and its political, scientific, and cultural consequences.

Californio to American: A Study in Cultural Change. cr.nps.gov/nr/twhp/wwwlps/les-sons/8californio/8californio.htm. National Park Service. U.S. Department of
the Interior. (Accessed 12/2/13).
Founded in 1790, Rancho Los Alamitos is one of the few surviving Spanish colonial
sites. Here teachers will find lesson plans and classroom materials to help students
understand how the Rancho and California changed as it passed from Spanish to
Mexican to American control.

MEDIA PICKS

California Up Close (Series). 5 DVDs. approx. 20 min. ea. Discovery Education
(store.discoveryeducation.com). 2006. $219.95. Includes: Native Americans
and European Explorers; Spanish California; Westward Expansion and State-hood; Modern California; California Today.
Gr 5-10–This comprehensive set looks at California's geography, history, culture,
and government, discussing its original indigenous inhabitants; the Europeans who
vied for it as a colonial prize; the Americans who seized it from Mexico, made it a
state, and developed its natural resources.

History Alive for Students: Living in Spanish Colonial America. DVD. 22 min. Discov-ery Education (store.discoveryeducation.com). 2000. $39.95.
Gr 4-8–Living-history footage illustrates the construction and operation of the Cal-

ifornia missions, showing how the crops and industries of the self-sustaining missions became the foundation of California's later development even as they transformed the culture and livelihood of the region's Native Americans.

Pioneer Spirit: Wagon Trails and the Oregon Trail. DVD. 26 min. Prod. by Fabian-Babar. Dist. by Discovery Education (store.discoveryeducation.com). 2001. $59.95. Gr 5-8–Maps, period illustrations, and living-history footage illustrate this comprehensive history of the early Pacific Northwest. Topics include the international competition for the region, the lucrative fur trade and missionary outreach that opened it for settlement, and the flood of Americans who quickly claimed it for the United States.

---

*Eds. Note: The full version of "California Bound"
can be accessed online at http://bit.ly/15nKv94*

· ·

—FOCUS ON—

POLITICS

We the People

By Jennifer S. Prince

*Jennifer S. Prince is a Youth Services Librarian at Buncombe County
Public Libraries, Asheville, NC.*

· ·

If the pundits and talking heads are to be believed, politics in America is dirty business. Lobbying, partisanship, pork-barrel spending, and mudslinging make up no small part of it. There is much more to politics, though. Beneath the necrotic layers of scandal and corruption are the birth-bright essentials of policy, governance, civics, and people. This collection of books, websites, and films attests to that with content, style, and format that are ideal for children and teens.

Using poetry, humor, history, science, fact, and fancy, these titles engage, enlighten, entertain, and inspire. In addition, new and archival photographs and stylistically diverse original paintings and drawings interpret and complement the texts with flair and vitality. Among these materials, a long-dead president enjoys a new sort of life thanks to a committed and creative group of scientists and historians; a camping trip inspires new laws, and a set of dusty paper dolls rekindles memories of White House life long ago. In short, politics is fleshed out in details that make it human and personal.

PRESIDENTS ARE PEOPLE TOO

Calkhoven, Laurie. I Grew Up to Be President. illus. by Rebecca Zomchek. Scholastic. 2011. pap. $8.99. ISBN 978-0-545-33152-4.

K-Gr 5–In this Washington-to-Obama collective biography, Calkhoven provides readers with succinct, cheerful accounts of presidential lives. The vital stats are here as well as facts that are strange, humorous, and, most of all, humanizing. Zomchek's stylish presentation juxtaposes presidential portraits with clever drawings of the presidents as boys. Informative and engaging.

Jurmain, Suzanne Tripp. Worst of Friends: Thomas Jefferson, John Adams, and the True Story of an American Feud. illus. by Larry Day. Dutton. 2011. Tr $16.99. ISBN 978-0-525-47903-1.

Gr 2-5–"Different as pickles and ice cream," Adams and Jefferson were America's original odd couple. Keeping the tone light, Jurmain explains why these close friends became enemies over the Constitution. Finely detailed watercolor illustrations are historically accurate with a little fun thrown in. 99 percent history + 1 percent whimsy = 100 percent awesomeness. Audio version available from Recorded Books.

Kalman, Maira. Looking at Lincoln. illus. by author. Penguin/Nancy Paulsen Bks. 2012. RTE $17.99. ISBN 978-0-399-24039-3.

Gr 2-5–Bold, emotionally resonant paintings flesh out the bare-bones account of Lincoln's life in this unusual and lovely homage. Kalman pairs facts with kindly guesses about Lincoln's thoughts on nicknames, dessert, and birthday presents. Somber reflections on war, slavery, and death are also included.

Katz, Susan. The President's Stuck in the Bathtub: Poems about the Presidents. illus. by Robert Neubecker. Clarion. 2012. RTE $17.99. ISBN 978-0-547-18221-6; ebook $17.99. ISBN 978-0-547-67783-5.

Gr 1-4–All 43 commanders-in-chief receive an individual poetic dousing in this lighthearted romp through our leaders' foibles, gaffes, embarrassments, and other unusual biographical details. Colorful, kinetic illustrations complement the spunky collection, and a brief explanatory note is appended to each poem. A fun supplement or lead-in to presidential biographies.

Kerley, Barbara. Those Rebels, John and Tom. illus. by Edwin Fotheringham. Scholastic. 2012. Tr $17.99. ISBN 978-0-545-22268-6.

Gr 2-5–This playful account shows how Adams's and Jefferson's opposing temperaments and talents were the winning combination to spur a recalcitrant congress into action and an ornery king into acquiescence. The illustrator toys with proportion and realism, filling the book with sight gags that interpret the text with wit and flair.

Krull, Kathleen & Paul Brewer. Lincoln Tells a Joke: How Laughter Saved the President (and the Country). illus. by Stacy Innerst. Harcourt. 2010. RTE. $17.ISBN 978-0-15-206639-0; ebook $17. ISBN 978-0-54-777019-2.

Gr 2-4–Lincoln faced enormous challenges personally and politically. In this readable biography, the authors complement key events with quips that demonstrate his keen sense of humor and love of language. Exaggerated acrylic illustrations match the folksy tone, while thick, slightly uneven brushstrokes add a timeworn appearance.

Mcclafferty, Carla Killough. The Many Faces of George Washington: Remaking a Presidential Icon. Carolrhoda. 2011. RTE $20.95. ISBN 978-0-7613-5608-0; ebook $15.71. ISBN 978-0-7613-7157-1.

Gr 6 Up–Blending science and history, McClafferty describes how professionals from several fields created three life-size models of Washington as he looked when he was a surveyor (age 19), an army general (age 45), and U.S. President (age 57). Dozens of color photographs document the process. Corresponding facts about Washington's life flesh out the illuminating narrative.

Mcnamara, Margaret. George Washington's Birthday: A Mostly True Tale. illus. by Barry Blitt. Random/Schwartz & Wade Bks, 2012. Tr $17.99. ISBN 978-0-375-84499-7; PLB $20.99. ISBN 978-0-375-94458-1.

Gr 1-4–Young George wakes up on the morning of his seventh birthday expecting but receiving no special notice from his family. As the tall tale plays out, McNamara includes elegantly trimmed sidebars with information confirming or supplanting events presented in the story. The watercolor illustrations, a blend of whimsy and realism, provide a perfect balance.

⌐
475.3 **National Children's Book And Literacy Alliance.** Our White House: Looking in, Looking Out.
○ illus. Candlewick. 2008. RTE $29.99. ISBN 978-0-7636-2067-7; pap. $14.99.
ISBN 978-0-7636-4609-7.

Gr 3-8–More than 100 children's and YA authors and illustrators add their voices to those of presidents and First Ladies to illuminate the history of the White House, past and present. Through poems, stories, memoirs, conversations, and colorful full-page illustrations, everyday life and special occasions are made vivid and compelling.

Rhatigan, Joe. White House Kids: The Perks, Pleasures, Problems, and Pratfalls of the Presidents' Children. illus. by Jay Shinn. Charlesbridge. 2012. Tr $14.95. ISBN 978-1-936140-80-0; ebook $9.99. ISBN 978-1-60734-472-8.

Gr 4-5–Iconic red, white, and blue graphics—archival photos and colorful original drawings—combine with anecdotes that recount life in the spotlight, the White House as a playground, and the pros and cons of growing up there. Impeccably researched, informative, and fun.

E **Smith, Lane.** John, Paul, George, & Ben. illus. by author. Hyperion. 2006. RTE $16.99. ISBN 978-0-7868-4893-5.

Gr 2-5–Smith spins a few outlandish backstories for some of America's founding fathers. Why was Paul Revere so good at yelling? What did Ben Franklin's friends think of his pithy sayings? Pen-and-ink drawings combine with collage to create appropriately zany illustrations. DVD and audio version available from Weston Woods.

ⓒ **Townsend, Michael.** Where Do Presidents Come From? And Other Presidential Stuff of Super Great Importance. Dial. Sept. 2012. Tr $14.99. ISBN 978-0-803-73748-8.

Gr 2-5–Vibrant cartoons and a steady stream of visual and verbal jokes enliven the text in this graphic novel that describes the origin of the American presidency, how the president is elected, what the job entails, the function of the White House, and life for the men once their terms are up.

YOU DON'T HAVE TO BE PRESIDENT TO GET INVOLVED

⌐ **Bruel, Nick.** Bad Kitty for President. illus. by author. Roaring Book. 2012. Tr $13.99.
Fɪc ISBN 978-1-59643-669-5; pap. $6.99. ISBN 978-1-2500-101-6-2.

Gr 2-4–Bad Kitty is running for president of the Neighborhood Cat Club. It's up to the narrator to educate the candidate about primaries, endorsements, campaigning, ethics, ads, debates, and voting. Bruel squeezes in lots of sound facts as Bad Kitty turns every election expectation on its head, while his integral black-and-white drawings are wittily expressive.

Clark, Catherine. How Not to Run for President. Egmont USA. 2012. Tr $15.99. ISBN 978-1-60684-101-3; ebook $15.99. ISBN 978-1-60684-302-4.

Gr 5–8–When a 12-year-old kid from Ohio saves the life of a presidential candidate, he finds himself swept up in a political blitz of campaigning and TV appearances. Events take an even more interesting turn when Aaron is asked to run as vice president. An entertaining and plausible read about national and local politics from a child's point of view.

Dipucchio, Kelly. Grace for President. illus. by LeUyen Pham. Hyperion. 2008. Tr $15.99. ISBN 978-0-7868-3919-3.

Gr 2–5–When eager Grace Campbell vies with super-student Thomas Cobb for class president, the children learn how the electoral college works. While Thomas does little during the campaign, Grace embarks on a school-wide tour winning over voters with her can-do attitude and kindness. Full-color, animated illustrations add polish and pep.

Fitzgerald, Dawn. Soccer Chick Rules. Roaring Brook. 2006. Tr $16.95. ISBN 978-1-596-43137-9; pap. $7.99. ISBN 978-0-312-37662-8.

Gr 5–8–Middle-school student Tess is passionate about soccer. When budget cuts threaten her school's sports program, she spearheads a movement to encourage voters to support a levy that would provide funding. Adolescent high jinks, sibling antagonism, and soccer details will resonate with young readers, while political activism adds an ennobling, but never preachy, dimension.

Fritz, Jean. Alexander Hamilton: The Outsider. illus. by Ian Schoenherr. Putnam. 2011. Tr $16.99. ISBN 978-0-399-25546-5; pap. $8.99. ISBN 978-0-142-41986-1; ebook $8.99. ISBN 978-1-101-47535-5.

Gr 5–9–Ambitious and intelligent, Hamilton lived under a cloud of suspicion due in large part to his irregular, turbulent youth. In this riveting biography, details of his military and political prowess blend with descriptions of colonial culture. Occasional, visually engaging black-and-white images enhance the text.

Malaspina, Ann. Heart on Fire: Susan B. Anthony Votes for President. illus. by Steve James. Albert Whitman. Sept. 2012. Tr $16.99. ISBN 978-0-8075-3188-4.

Gr 2-5–"Outrageous. Unbelievable. True." is the refrain in this stunning picture book about the uproar caused when Susan B. Anthony registered to vote and then actually voted. Word and image evoke the frisson of witnessing absurd injustice in a society that is veiled in modernity and culture. Incisive storytelling and luminous oil paintings make for a memorable, important read.

Smith, Lane. Madam President. illus. by author. Hyperion. 2008. RTE $16.99. ISBN 978-1-4231-0846-7.

Gr 2-5–An ambitious little girl imagines what it would be like to be president of the United States. Her imperfect, egotistical understanding of presidential privilege is at once lightly educational and hilarious. Stylized collage illustrations offer detailed insight into the girl's life and imagination. Audio version available from Weston Woods.

Winston, Sherri. President of the Whole Fifth Grade. Little, Brown. 2010. Tr $15.99. ISBN 978-0-316-11432-5; pap. $6.99. ISBN 978-0-316-11433-2; ebook $9.99. ISBN 978-0-316-12298-6.

Gr 3-5–Bright and friendly Brianna is a shoo-in for the office of president of the fifth grade until self-assured Jasmine moves to town. When she tries to undermine Brianna, Brianna must decide whether or not to respond in kind. The message is clear but not preachy. A light look at elementary-school shenanigans and politics.

Wong, Janet. Declaration of Interdependence: Poems for an Election Year. CreateSpace. 2012. pap. $7.99. ISBN 978-1-468-19191-2.

Gr 6 Up–These 20 poems cover an election year from the viewpoint of a teen who is not old enough to vote. The lean, incisive verses explore tolerance, free speech, campaign ads, winning and losing, equality, and more. The authentic voice and evocative insight make this collection a great choice for readers' theater.

POLITICS IN ACTION

Burgan, Michael. Political Parties. illus. by Charles Barnett III. (Cartoon Nation Series). Capstone. 2008. PLB $29.99. ISBN 978-1-4296-1334-7; pap. $7.95. ISBN 978-1-4296-1782-6.

Gr 2-5–Tongue ensconced firmly in cheek, this book explains the formation and evolution of the major political parties in America. Dynamic comic-book art enlivens descriptions of the spoils system, the electoral college, party presses, and much more. Lively, funny, and accurate.

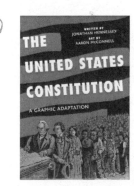

Hennessey, Jonathan. The United States Constitution: A Graphic Adaptation. illus. by Aaron McConnell. Farrar. 2008. pap. $16.95. ISBN 978-0-809-09470-7.
Gr 5 Up–Hennessey explains each article and amendment in laypeople's terms. The shadowy, surreal art depicts key moments in Constitutional history (trial of the Scottsboro boys, the Seneca Falls convention, etc.) and gives emotional weight to the straightforward analysis. Readers will want to have a copy of the full text of the Constitution handy.

Jules, Jacqueline. Unite or Die: How Thirteen States Became a Nation. illus. by Jef Czekaj. Charlesbridge. 2009. RTE $16.95. ISBN 978-1-58089-189-9; pap. $7.95. ISBN 978-1-58089-190-5.
Gr 2-5–Brimming with colorful, cartoon illustrations and simple text, this book uses the ubiquitous school play to describe the development of the U.S. Constitution. In a lighthearted but factual skit, kids act out the Convention's high-stakes bid to govern 13 recalcitrant states. Historically sound, easy to understand, and fun.

Morris-Lippman, Arlene. Presidential Races: Campaigning for the White House. (People's History Series). Twenty-First Century. 2012. PLB $33.26. ISBN 978-0-7613-7395-7.
Gr 6-8–A revision of *Presidential Races: The Battle for Power in the United States* (2008), this title ushers readers through the most dramatic, influential, and pivotal elections. Political cartoons and photos complement the text. The most substantive revision is the inclusion of the race between McCain and Obama. That addition alone warrants purchase.

Rosenstock, Barb. The Camping Trip That Changed America: Theodore Roosevelt, John Muir, and Our National Parks. illus. by Mordecai Gerstein. Dial. 2012. RTE $16.99. ISBN 978-0-8037-3710-5.
Gr 1-4–Brimming with fun and fact, this book recounts a 1903 camping trip in which Roosevelt asked Muir to convince him that conservation mattered. Soon after the trip, Roosevelt enacted legislation that marked the nascency of America's national park system. Ink and watercolor illustrations, with a studied messiness, match the folksy tone of the text.

Schanzer, Rosalyn. George vs. George: The American Revolution as Seen from Both Sides. illus. by author. National Geographic. 2004. Tr $16.95. ISBN 978-0-7922-7349-3; PLB $25.90. ISBN 978-0-7922-6999-1; pap. $6.95. ISBN 978-1-4263-0042-4.

Gr 4-8–To George Washington, King George III was a tyrant. To King George III, George Washington was a traitor. Gleaning from hundreds of sources to flesh out text and illustrations, Schanzer presents a vivid example of how there are two sides to every story—a fact that is easy to overlook in politics. Well told and gorgeously illustrated.

ON THE WEB

For Teachers

Kids Voting USA. kidsvotingusa.org. Kids Voting USA. Topeka, KS. (Accessed 7/25/12). Free and easy registration allows educators of grades K-12 access to a range of civically and politically themed activities. The lesson objective, list of materials needed, detailed instructions, and time required are provided for each activity.

For Students

Annenberg Classroom: Resources for Excellent Civics Education. www.annenberg classroom.org. The Leonore Annenberg Institute for Civics. Philadelphia, PA. (Accessed 7/25/12).

Gr 5 Up–A wealth of well-conceived podcasts, lesson plans, time lines, and videos on the Constitution and branches of government is easily accessible here. Of particular note is *Key Constitutional Concepts*, a 60-minute, 3-part video presented with a snappy narrative, dynamic montages, and dashes of humor. Accompanying teaching guides are an added bonus.

Congress for Kids. congressforkids.net. The Dirksen Congressional Center. Pekin, IL. (Accessed 7/25/12).

Gr 4-8–With Uncle Sam leading the way, students journey through colorful, engaging, and interactive presentations about the history of the federal government. Includes games and quizzes.

Kids.gov. kids.usa.gov. USA.gov. (Accessed 7/25/12).

K-Gr 8–A finely curated portal to .edu and .gov websites featuring games, quizzes, and colorful presentations about a wide variety of topics, including government, social studies, and history, this site offers an informative (and free) "How to Become President of the United States" poster.

MEDIA PICKS

American Government for Children (Series). 6 DVDs. 23 min. ea. with tchr's. guide. Prod. by Schlessinger Media. Dist. by Library Video Co. 2001. $179.70 ser., $29.95 ea. Includes: American Citizenship; The History of American Government; Federal, State & Local Government; A History of the Presidency; The Three Branches of Government; What Is Government?

K-Gr 4–The series begins by answering the question, "What Is Government?" Various types of governments are discussed and contrasted with democracies. There's an overview *Federal, State, & Local Government.* Two programs concentrate on the history of the presidency and our government. *American Citizenship* explains our rights and responsibilities. In each video, a group of young people conduct research on the general topic. Interviews with government officials and others bring the concepts to life. Historical documents, photos, and video clips are included.

The American Presidents 1890-1945: The Emergence of Modern America/The Great Depression & WWII. DVD. approx. 45 min. with tchr's. guide. Disney Educational. 2010. ISBN 1-59753-253-3. $29.99.
The American Presidents 1945-2010: Postwar & Contemporary United States. DVD. approx. 80 min. with tchr's guide. Disney Educational. 2010. ISBN 1-59753-254-1. $29.99.
Gr 3-8–The presidencies of Theodore Roosevelt through Franklin D. Roosevelt and Harry Truman through Barack Obama are covered. Short biographies present defining characteristics of each president as well as his challenges and accomplishments. Major issues are addressed in successive presidencies. Diverse viewpoints are articulated by professors, politicians, military officers, political commentators, and others.

Getting to Know the U.S. Presidents: Abraham Lincoln. DVD. 22 min. Getting to Know. 2011. ISBN 978-0-9828-8035-7. $39.95.
Gr 1-6–Mike Venezia takes factual information and makes it personal, while tossing in funny asides through hilarious cartoon illustrations in this production based on his book (Childrens Press, 2005). Lincoln narrates the story of his life with warmth and humor. Information about the causes and impact of the Civil War and the issue of slavery is presented. Historical photos and artwork augment content. Other titles focus on Washington, Adams, and Jefferson.

Otto Runs for President. DVD. 12 min. Weston Woods. 2008. ISBN 978-0-545-
10650-4: $59.95.

PreS-Gr 4–It's election time at Barkadelphia School in this story (Scholastic, 2008)
by Rosemary Wells. Tiffany, the pretty and popular poodle, and Charles, the bull-
dog sports star, are getting lots of financial help from their parents as they run a
no-holds-barred campaign. Things get ugly as accusations fly and the two try every
campaign trick to woo voters. Meanwhile, Otto observes that the candidates are
only thinking of themselves, and he decides to run against them.

Eds. note: The full version of "We the People" can be accessed
online at http://bit.ly/16nVEGL

· ·

—FOCUS ON—

CIVIL RIGHTS

Everyday Heroes

By Rhona Campbell

Rhona Campbell is a teacher-librarian at Georgetown Day School in Washington,
DC.

· ·

In May 1963, people round our country turned on their televisions to the
sight of children being viciously assaulted with fire hoses and snarling
dogs by uniformed grown men, their faces twisted with hatred. The violence in Birmingham, Alabama, stirred a swelling of national conscience and
raised questions demanding an answer: Do we really believe that "all men
are created equal"? What would our country look like if we really did? What
has to change to make that dream a reality?

Until recently, most books for children about the Civil Rights Movement focused on the great leaders. Now, authors and illustrators are using multiple lenses, choosing to illuminate the inner workings of a popu-
list revolution in which many people, with differing beliefs, made difficult
choices. Historical fiction and poetry delve empathetically into motivations,

situations, and dilemmas. Enticing nonfiction presents a variety of primary sources representing multiple viewpoints, asking readers to compare and contrast versions of reality, draw their own inferences, find personal meaning, and examine the art of history-telling.

These books about the Civil Rights era contain universal themes: How do we recognize and address our own prejudices? How do we make social change happen? How do we find the strength to overcome adversity and do what we know to be right? How can one person change the world? Give these titles to students so that they may start to answer these questions for themselves.

PANNING THE SCENE
Background, Overviews, Introductions

Osborne, Linda Barrett. Miles to Go for Freedom: Segregation and Civil Rights in the Jim Crow Era. Abrams. 2012. RTE $24.95. ISBN 978-1-4197-0020-0.

Gr 6-10—Osborne thoroughly supports her historical examination of segregation with well-chosen quotations, rare photographs, ephemera, and other visual information from the Library of Congress. This cleanly written history of the Jim Crow era is ideal for anyone studying the times, or simply interested in our shared past. A highly readable, substantive title.

Pinkney, Andrea Davis. Sit-In: How Four Friends Stood Up by Sitting Down. illus. by Brian Pinkney. Little, Brown. 2010. Tr $16.99. ISBN 978-0-316-07016-4. Gr 2-5–With the 1960 Greensboro Woolworth counter sit-in as a central example and food as a metaphor, Pinkney's highly readable poetic phrases relate how ordinary people's nonviolent actions eventually led to integration. Brian Pinkney's buoyant color washes with vibrant ink drawings enhance the spirited tone of his wife's words.

Ramsey, Calvin A. Ruth and the Green Book. illus. by Floyd Cooper. Carolrhoda. 2010. RTE $16.95. ISBN 978-0-7613-5255-6.

Gr 1-4–A young African American girl uses the Green Book to find black-friendly businesses on her family's 1950 car trip from Chicago to rural Alabama, easing the pain of her first encounters with Jim Crow. Cooper's art, using a grainy, subdued palette that subtly evokes historical photographs, supports this understated but interesting slice of history.

Shange, Ntozake. We Troubled the Waters. illus. by Rod Brown. HarperCollins/Amistad. 2009. Tr $16.99. ISBN 978-0-06-133735-2; ebook $11.99. ISBN 978-0-06-206563-6.
Gr 6 Up–Shange's spare, dialect-strong poems are vivid, emotional snapshots of the Jim Crow South from a black perspective. They leave plenty of thought-provoking, unspoken ideas between the lines. Together with Brown's photograph-inspired muralistic oil paintings, this powerful book invokes personal reactions to historical wrongs.

Stotts, Stuart. We Shall Overcome: A Song That Changed the World. foreword by Pete Seeger. illus. by Terrance Cummings. Clarion. 2010. RTE $18. ISBN 978-0-547-18210-0.
Gr 4 Up–The anthem of the Civil Rights Movement steadied and fortified the righteous. Here is a mini-ethnomusicological study of the song, from its origins through its role at many dangerous and important protests. Archival images, strong poster-art-inspired red/black/white artwork, and a CD accompany the story of the song's journey.

Watkins, Angela Farris. My Uncle Martin's Words for America. illus. by Eric Velasquez. Abrams. 2011. RTE $19.95. ISBN 978-1-4197-0022-4.
K-Gr 4–In the grand tradition of deifying King, this title works well as a lap-read companion to Doreen Rappaport's *Martin's Big Words* (Hyperion, 2001). Bold text emphasizes the simple concepts of King's satyagraha philosophy while taking on a more complete, but age-appropriate, history of the movement. Bright oil-painted portraits backed by stars and stripes lend a patriotic tone.

ZOOMING IN
· · · · · · · · · · · · · · ·
Places & Events

Bausum, Ann. Marching to the Mountaintop: How Poverty, Labor Fights, and Civil Rights Set the Stage for Martin Luther King, Jr.'s Final Hours. National Geographic. 2012. Tr $19.95. ISBN 978-1-4263-0939-7; PLB $28.90. ISBN 978-1-4263-0940-3; ebook $19.95. ISBN 978-1-4263-0945-8.
Gr 6 Up–When the Civil Rights Movement arrived in Memphis, Tennessee, in 1968, the volatile mix of poverty, racial discrimination, and the black community's

own splintered loyalties came to a boil. This behind-the-scenes exposé sheds light on a specific place and time usually overshadowed by the subsequent assassination of King at the Lorraine Hotel.

Brimner, Larry Dane. Birmingham Sunday. Boyds Mill/Calkins Creek. 2010. RTE $17.95. ISBN 978-1-59078-613-0.
Gr 6 Up–Brimner homes in on the racially charged atmosphere of Birmingham in 1963 by hooking readers with details about the four victims of the Sixteenth Street Baptist Church bombing. These 48 pages, packed with photographs and sidebars of related information, reveal the shocking extent to which raw violence and danger were prevalent.

Conkling, Winifred. Sylvia & Aki. Tricycle. 2011. Tr $16.99. ISBN 978-1-58246-337-7; PLB $19.99. ISBN 978-1-58246-438-1.
Gr 4-6–Meet Sylvia and Aki, two real Southern Californian girls facing government-supported discrimination during World War II. Extrapolating from interviews, Conkling has crafted an alternating-narrator novel that compares and contrasts experiences by Americans of Mexican and Japanese heritage. This title reminds readers that the Civil Rights Movement wasn't just about inequities faced by African Americans.

Dudley, David L. Caleb's Wars. Clarion. 2011. Tr $16.99. ISBN 978-0-547-23997-2; ebook $11.99. ISBN 978-0-547-53420-6.
Gr 7 Up–In this novel of World War II-era rural Georgia, Caleb, a 15-year-old African American, chafes at the ways his family and community take Jim Crow for granted, despite his brother's service in the U.S. Army. Getting to know a German POW assigned to work with him intensifies Caleb's determination to claim his dignity.

Evans, Shane W. We March. illus. by author. Roaring Brook/A Neal Porter Bk. 2012. Tr $16.99. ISBN 978-1-59643-539-1; eook $9.99. ISBN 978-1-46681-084-6.
PreS-Gr 4–Evans's expansive, richly colored, simplistic paintings depict a young African American family preparing for and attending the 1963 March on Washington. With carefully chosen, spare language, this simple book powerfully re-creates the event. Brief back matter provides much-needed context.

Kittinger, Jo S. Rosa's Bus: The Ride to Civil Rights. illus. by Steven Walker. Boyds Mill/Calkins Creek. 2010. Tr $17.95. ISBN 978-1-59078-722-9.
Gr 1-4–A fresh twist on the familiar tale of Rosa Parks's defiance and the Montgomery Bus Boycott, with straightforward, simple storytelling, focuses on the historical

nature of the bus itself. Walker's bright oil paintings balance the text and mood throughout. Endnotes offer additional information for the inevitable questions from a read-aloud audience.

Levine, Kristin. The Lions of Little Rock. Putnam. 2012. Tr $16.99. ISBN 978-0-399-

25644-8; pap. $7.99. ISBN 978-0-1-424-2435-3; ebook $10.99. ISBN 978-1-101-55044-1.

Gr 5-8–This novel depicts 1958 Little Rock, roiling in racial tension in the wake of the Little Rock Nine. Desperately shy Marley befriends a new classmate at her still-segregated white middle school. When it's discovered that her new friend is actually a black girl passing for white, the two must decide how important their friendship is. Audio version available from Listening Library.

Partridge, Elizabeth. Marching for Freedom: Walk Together, Children, and Don't You Grow Weary. Viking. 2009. Tr $19.99. ISBN 978-0-670-01189-6; ebook $16.99. ISBN 978-1-101-15097-9.

Gr 6 Up–From Bloody Sunday to the March on Montgomery, this nonfiction book presents the events of the summer of 1965 in Selma, Alabama, in a photo-journalistic story arc, complete with real-life teenage "characters" found through exten-

sive interviews. Well-chosen, striking photographs contextualize the chronological retelling, supporting the real-life drama. Audio version available from Brilliance Audio.

Scattergood, Augusta. Glory Be. Scholastic. 2012. Tr $16.99. ISBN 978-0-545-33180-7. Gr 4-7–In 1964 when her small Mississippi town closes Glory's beloved swimming pool to avoid integration, the naive white 11-year-old takes a stand. Glory's story, focusing primarily on members of the white community, compares and contrasts the small actions and inactions of different characters.

Tougas, Shelley. Little Rock Girl 1957: How a Photograph Changed the Fight for Integration. (Captured History Series). Compass Point. 2012. PLB $33.99. ISBN 978-0-7565-4440-9; pap. $8.95. ISBN 978-0-7565-4512-3. Gr 4-8–The focus here is the shocking photograph of 15-year-old Elizabeth Eckford being viciously jeered by a white peer as she and her fellow black students integrated Little Rock Central High School in 1957. Tougas explains the context of the photograph and how the iconic image affected history.

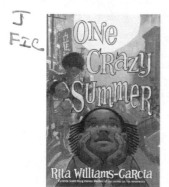

J FIC

Williams-Garcia, Rita. One Crazy Summer. HarperCollins/ Amistad. 2010. Tr $15.99. ISBN 978-0-06-076088-5; pap. $6.99. ISBN 978-0-06-076088-5; ebook $6.99. ISBN 978-0-06-196667-5.

Gr 5-9–Spending the summer of 1968 at a Black Panther summer camp is not what the three African American sisters of this novel intend when they visit their estranged mother in Oakland, California, but what they learn about racial identity and pride changes their lives forever. Audio version available from Recorded Books.

PORTRAITS
Featured Faces

Brimner, Larry Dane. Black & White: The Confrontation between Reverend Fred L. Shuttlesworth and Eugene "Bull" Connor. Boyds Mills/Calkins Creek. 2011. RTE $16.95. ISBN 978-1-59078-766-3.

Gr 6 Up–A fascinating photo-journalistic, two-person biography about the obstinate men who led black and white factions against each other in 1960s Birmingham, Alabama, not only showcases the important role played by the oft-overshadowed Rev. Fred L. Shuttleworth, but also reveals how extremist factions overrode the more moderate voices of other Birmingham residents.

Hoose, Phillip. Claudette Colvin: Twice Toward Justice. Farrar/Melanie Kroupa Bks. 2009. Tr $19.99. ISBN 978-0-374-31322-7; pap. $9.99. ISBN 978-0-312-66105-2; ebook $9.99. ISBN 978-1-429-94821-0.

Gr 6 Up–Hoose's slice of little-known history introduces readers to Claudette Colvin, the teenager who did exactly what Rosa Parks became so famous for nine months later. However, Colvin was marginalized by the very same famous adults (the NAACP, Dr. King, etc.) readers have been taught to revere. Guaranteed to spark a "That's not fair!" response.

Jeffrey, Gary. Medgar Evers and the NAACP. illus. by Nick Spender. (A Graphic History of the Civil Rights Movement). Gareth Stevens. 2012. PLB $23.95. ISBN 978-1-4339-7495-3; pap. $8.15. ISBN 978-1-4339-7496-0; ebook $23.95. ISBN 978-1-4339-7498-4.

Gr 3–7–The richly colored, pamphlet-size graphic novels in this series are excellent fodder for reluctant readers. This old-fashioned dramatic comic-book retelling of the 1963 assassination of Mississippi Civil Rights leader Medgar Evers attributes a hero's due to the man's pride and perseverance. A brief textual preface and afterword frame the action.

Pinkney, Andrea Davis. Hand in Hand: Ten Black Men Who Changed America. illus. by Brian Pinkney. Hyperion/Disney. 2012. Tr $19.99. ISBN 978-1-4231-4257-7.

Gr 4 Up–In this compilation intended for sequential reading, Andrea Pinkney's comfortable storytelling style showcases the intelligence, perseverance, and leadership of 10 black men from Benjamin Banneker through Barack Obama. A poem and a full-page lively facial portrait preface each fascinating biography; Brian Pinkney's smaller, paint-washed scenes are also inset throughout.

Stokes, John A. with Lois Wolfe & Herman Viola. Students on Strike: Jim Crow, Civil Rights, Brown, and Me. National Geographic. 2008. Tr $15.95. ISBN 978-1-4263-0153-7; PLB $23.90. ISBN 978-1-4263-0154-4.

Gr 5-9–In 1951, Stokes and other black students in Farmville, Virginia, organized against the city to request a high school building as nice as the one the white students attended. Reading Stokes's chatty style is like hanging out with a guy who's reminiscing about the accidentally remarkable things he did when he was young.

Teitelbaum, Michael & Lewis Helfand. Martin Luther King, Jr.: Let Freedom Ring. illus. by Sankha Banerjee. (Campfire Graphic Novels Series). Campfire. Jan. 2013. pap. $12.99. ISBN 978-93-80028-69-9

Gr 4-6–Drawn reproductions of iconic news photographs alternate with text boxes and imagined private moments as the biographers portray age-appropriate aspects of this very public figure's life. A straightforward graphic-novel biography, each page rich with color, detail, and nicely balanced design.

MEDIA PICKS

Freedom Riders: John Lewis and Jim Zwerg on the Front Lines of the Civil Rights Movement. **Ann Bausum.** 2 cassettes or 2 CDs. 1:30 hrs. Recorded Books. 2008. cassette: ISBN 978-1-4281-8683-5, CD: ISBN 978-1-4281-8688-0. $25.75.

Gr 5-9–Bausum's powerful book (National Geographic, 2005) about the experiences of John Lewis and Jim Zwerg during the Freedom Rides of the early 1960s is narrated by Cecelia Riddett, whose impassioned reading emphasizes the brutal facts of how these men risked their lives to take on the racist practices of interstate bus travel.

March On! The Day My Brother Martin Changed the World. DVD. 18 min. Weston Woods. 2008. ISBN 978-0-545-10645-0. $59.95; CD with hardcover book. ISBN 978-0-545-10689-4: $29.95.

Gr 2-7–Christine King Farris recalls her brother, Martin Luther King, Jr., in this evocative picture book (Scholastic, 2008) focusing on the 1963 March on Washington where he gave his famous "I Have a Dream" speech. Lynn Whitfield reads the story with great emotion, bringing viewers to the National Mall to witness this historic event, while London Ladd's realistic illustrations and historical photographs are scanned.

The Other Side. DVD. 8 min. Weston Woods. 2012. ISBN 978-0-545-44754-6. $59.95; CD, ISBN 978-0-545-44759-1: $12.95; CD with hardcover book, ISBN 978-0-545-44811-6: $29.95.

K-Gr 4–Clover, an African American girl, lives on one side of the fence and Annie, a white girl, lives on the other side. Set during segregation, this story shows how the children are drawn to test those artificial boundaries that separate and classify. Jacqueline Woodson's deceptively simple, yet powerfully evocative story is supported by E. B. Lewis's wonderful watercolor illustrations.

The Rise and Fall of Jim Crow. 4 DVDs. approx. 4 hrs. California Newsreel. 2002. $24.95.

Gr 9 Up–After the end of the Civil War, many Southern states refused to grant freed slaves equality with whites. This outstanding production, spanning the years from 1865 to 1954, shows how legal segregation shaped the social, political, and legal history of the period. Historical figures and everyday citizens relate the story of their struggles.

Rosa. DVD. 14 min. with tchr's. guide. Weston Woods. 2007. ISBN 978-0-545-04257-4. $59.95; CD with hardcover book, ISBN 978-0-545-04261-1: $29.95.

Gr 2-5–Rosa Parks's legacy lives on in Nikki Giovanni's beautiful Caldecott Honor picture book (Holt, 2005). The crisp text is read by the author while Bryan Collier's collage illustrations are scanned, as well as a few of his illustrations from Doreen Rappaport's *Martin's Big Words* (Hyperion, 2001; Weston Woods) and archival photographs.

White Water. DVD. 9 min. with tchr's. guide. Nutmeg Media. 2012. ISBN 1-933938-88-9. $49.95.

K-Gr 3–In White Water, based on Michael S. Bandy and Eric Stein's picture book of the same name, a young African American boy notices segregation's inequities. He's especially struck by the drinking fountains—one for Whites and another for Coloreds. Tony Fragale narrates the first-person story as the boy devises a plan to find out what "white water" tastes like. Inspired by actual events, this work brings home the reality of segregation.

ON THE WEB

American Experience. Eyes on the Prize. America's Civil Rights Movement 1954-1985. www.pbs.org/wgbh/amex/eyesontheprize/story/index.html. PBS Online/WGBH. (Accessed 11/25/12).

Gr 6 Up–The webpages accompanying this 14-hour documentary of the Civil Rights Movement are organized chronologically by topic and feature many primary sources, including audio/video clips, photographs, maps, and more. Text heavy, this is best for middle or high school students.

BCRI Resource Center Gallery. rg.bcri.org/gallery. Birmingham Civil Rights Institute. (Accessed 11/25/12).

Gr 4-8–With an attractive design and plenty of simply organized, flashy, well-produced videos, this interactive gallery of video clips and audio makes a great introduction to the era, particularly to the events in Birmingham. Includes an overview, oral histories, a time line, and other resources.

Eds. note: The full version of "Everyday People"
can be accessed online at http://bit.ly/1baVbv8

World History

○ **Bogacki, Tomek.** The Champion of Children: The Story of Janusz Korczak. 40 pp. Farrar/
Foster 2009. ISBN 978-0-374-34136-7.

With simple, unadorned prose thoughtfully positioned within the soft acrylic illustrations that fill the pages, Bogacki describes the life of Korczak, a tireless advocate
for children's rights. The book ends with Korczak's deportation to Treblinka with
his orphans, and while the pictures are honest in depicting even this journey to the
death camps, their gentleness inspires empathy rather than horror.
*Individual Biographies; Children; Doctors; Korczak, Janusz; History, Modern–Holocaust;
Jews; Poland*

J 387.2 **Brown, Don.** All Stations! Distress!: April 15, 1912: The Day the Titanic Sank. 64 pp.
Roaring Brook/Flash Point 2008. ISBN 978-1-59643-222-2 PE ISBN 978-1-
59643-644-2. Actual Times series.

Brown recounts the complicated, compact last moments of the *Titanic*'s only
voyage. The glory of the book is in Brown's moody watercolors done with a
brush dipped in stardust and frozen mist; they reach a terrifying crescendo as
the ship upends before the final dive. The tale closes with some information
about the survivors' later lives. Bib.
Modern History; Titanic (Steamship); Disasters; Vehicles–Ships; Shipwrecks

○ 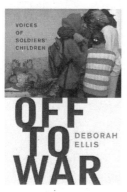 **Ellis, Deborah.** Off to War: Voices of Soldiers' Children. 176 pp.
Groundwood (House of Anansi Press) 2008. ISBN 978-
0-88899-894-1 PE ISBN 978-0-88899-895-8.

Ellis interviews American and Canadian children whose parents have been deployed to Iraq or Afghanistan. Chapters
begin with an introduction; the rest is told in the children's
words. Especially interesting is their honesty about what happens when the parent comes home. Readers will empathize
with these young people whose lives have been upended by
circumstances beyond their control. Websites. Ind.
*Families/Children/and Sexuality; Family–Parent and child; War; Soldiers; Children's
writings; History, Modern–Iraq War; Afghanistan*

Freedman, Russell. The War to End All Wars: World War I. 170 pp. Clarion 2010. ISBN 978-0-547-02686-2 PE ISBN 978-0-544-02171-6. *Also Y*

With an abundance of historical photographs and a characteristically lucid, well-organized text, Freedman documents the history of the First World War: from its tangled beginnings, through years of stalemate, to the collapse of empires and uneasy peace, and ending with a brief description of the rise of Hitler. Freedman's narrative, dedicated to his WWI veteran father, is dramatic and often heart-wrenching. Bib., ind.
Modern History; History, Modern–World War I

Freedman, Russell. Who Was First?: Discovering the Americas. 88 pp. Clarion 2007. ISBN 978-0-618-66391-0.

Freedman demonstrates how North and South America have been discovered and settled over and over since the Stone Age. In lively, graceful prose, he invites readers to ponder serious historical questions. Straightforward explanations of various historical theories include evidence for and against their validity. The book's design adds to its appeal, with plenty of color, ample white space, and carefully chosen illustrations. Bib., ind.
Geography and Exploration; North America

Halls, Kelly Milner. Saving the Baghdad Zoo: A True Story of Hope and Heroes. 64 pp. Greenwillow (HarperCollins Children's Books Group) 2010. ISBN 978-0-06-177202-3 LE ISBN 978-0-06-177200-9. Photographs by William Sumner.

This moving photo essay reveals how Americans and Iraqis, with assistance from international animal welfare groups, worked together to relocate and rehabilitate zoo animals abandoned in their cages when the war began. Today the reopened Baghdad Zoo provides sanctuary for animal inhabitants and human visitors alike. A strong thread of emotion pulls together the animals' stories. Bib., ind.
Natural History; Iraq; Zoos; Animals–Zoo animals; Baghdad (Iraq); War

Hopkinson, Deborah. Titanic: Voices from the Disaster. 290 pp. Scholastic 2012. ISBN 978-0-545-11674-9 PE ISBN 978-0-545-43677-9.

Hopkinson provides young readers with a basic introduction to the event without overdramatizing, drawing unwarranted conclusions, or prolonging the ordeal. Her "characters," real survivors whose voices relay many of the subsequent events, include crew members as well as travelers in first, second, and third class. Chapter notes, sources, archival photos, a time-

line, short biographies of those mentioned, and more are included. Bib., glos., ind.
Modern History; Titanic (Steamship); Disasters; Shipwrecks

Krull, Kathleen. Kubla Khan: The Emperor of Everything. 48 pp. Viking 2010. ISBN 978-0-670-01114-8. Illustrated by Robert Byrd.

The thirteenth-century Mongol ruler was no barbarian; Krull presents a nuanced view of his surprisingly tolerant regime. Byrd's tapestry-like ink and watercolor illustrations reflect the broad scope of the Khan's reach and his receptive mind. Though Krull admits in an afterword that "information about Kubla Khan is sketchy," she draws on what is known in order to pull a real man from the legend.
Individual Biographies; Kings, queens, and rulers; Kublai Khan; Mongol Empire; China, Ancient

Layson, Annelex Hofstra. Lost Childhood: My Life in a Japanese Prison Camp During World War II. 112 pp. National (National Geographic Books) 2008. ISBN 978-1-4263-0321-0 LE ISBN 978-1-4263-0322-7. With Herman J. Viola.

In 1942, four-year-old Annelex, her mother, and grandmother, Dutch citizens living in the Dutch East Indies, were interned by the Japanese. Recapturing a child's-eye view, Layson narrates simply, letting events speak for themselves. With its similarities and contrasts to Japanese internment in the U.S. and to Holocaust accounts, this is a worthy addition to the World War II canon. Timeline.
Individual Biographies; Indonesia; Women–Autobiographies; Autobiographies; Concentration camps; History, Modern–World War II; Japan; Women–Biographies; Prisons and prisoners

Metselaar, Menno and van der Rol, Ruud. Anne Frank: Her Life in Words and Pictures. 216 pp. Roaring Brook/Flash Point 2009. ISBN 978-1-59643-546-9 PE ISBN 978-1-59643-547-6. Translated by Arnold J. Pomerans.

The beginning of this extraordinary little book functions essentially as a family photo album. In the 1942–1944 ("In hiding") section, the authors use diary excerpts, augmented with helpful explanations, while the photographs go inside the Secret Annex. The book's conclusion describes Anne's tragic death and the publication of her diary. Goosebump-inducingly immediate, it's a treasure for everyone inspired by Anne's story. Glos.
Individual Biographies; Books in translation; Women–Biographies; Jews; Women–Jews; Frank, Anne; History, Modern–Holocaust; Amsterdam (Netherlands); Diaries

O'Brien, Patrick. The Mutiny on the Bounty. 40 pp. Walker 2007. ISBN 978-0-8027-9587-8. O'Brien introduces the *HMS Bounty* to young readers in this generously illustrated volume that includes double-page spreads, full-page illustrations, and quarter- and half-page frames reminiscent of graphic novels. Potentially unfamiliar words frequently have both brief descriptions and spot illustrations. Accessible and clear, this straightforward account allows young readers a glimpse of an event that is part of our cultural literacy.

General and World History; Cartoons and comics; Sea stories; Vehicles–Ships; Sailors

Ross, Stewart. Into the Unknown: How Great Explorers Found Their Way by Land, Sea, and Air. 96 pp. Candlewick 2011. ISBN 978-0-7636-4948-7 PE ISBN 978-0-7636-6992-8. Illustrated by Stephen Biesty.

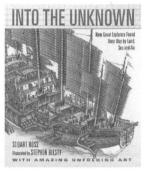

This remarkable book presents fourteen historical explorations, from Pytheas the Greek's three-thousand-years-ago voyage to Armstrong, Aldrin, and Collins's moon shot, with the question "how did they *do* that?" as focus. Detailed cross sections, often displayed in foldout segments, diagram each mode of transportation; maps abound, also within foldout pages. The text diligently differentiates between fact and opinion. Bib., glos., ind.

Geography and Exploration; Toy and movable books; Transportation; Vehicles Ancient and Medieval History; Islamic Empire; Religion–Islam; Inventions and inventors

Schlitz, Laura Amy. Good Masters! Sweet Ladies!: Voices from a Medieval Village. 85 pp. Candlewick 2007. ISBN 978-0-7636-1578-9 PE ISBN 978-0-7636-4332-4. Illustrated by Robert Byrd.

Schlitz presents seventeen monologues and two dialogues about life in the Middle Ages. Rhythm and style vary, from breathless phrases describing a boar hunt to more light-hearted rhymes. Schlitz conveys information about class, attitudes, and social practices through the monologues, footnote-like sidebars, and six spreads titled "A Little Background." Byrd's pen-and-ink illustrations in opulent colors are pristine and elegant.

Performing Arts; Middle Ages; Plays; England

Siegal, Aranka. Memories of Babi. 116 pp. Farrar 2008. ISBN 978-0-374-39978-8. In these nine anecdotes, Siegal recalls summers on her grandmother's Ukrainian farm. Her experiences include cooking (recipes are appended), mushroom hunting, and feather plucking. Though the setting is pre-Holocaust, there's already tension between Christians and Jews; the book's last paragraph tells Babi's fate. Siegal is notably able to project characters vividly, to write simply without condescension, and to interweave themes without preaching.

Individual Biographies; Hungary; Women–Biographies; Farms and farm life; Family–Grandmothers; Women–Jews; Ukraine; Jews; Women–Autobiographies; Autobiographies

Sís, Peter. The Wall: Growing Up behind the Iron Curtain. 56 pp. Farrar/Foster 2007. ISBN 978-0-374-34701-7.

Born in 1949, as Czechoslovakia fell under Soviet domination, Sís evokes the childhood of an artist in a country of growing restrictions. Brief main text describes Sís's experiences, and small captions illuminate the thumbnail pictures of conditions in the country. Media and color choices throughout are expert and telling. It's a surprisingly comprehensive portrait of an era and an artist..

Individual Biographies; Communism; Czechoslovakia; Autobiographies; Illustrators; Authors; Czech Americans

Also Adult Non Fic 943.7 Sis [handwritten]

Skrypuch, Marsha Forchuk. Last Airlift: A Vietnamese Orphan's Rescue from War. 110 pp. Pajama Press 2012. ISBN 978-0-9869495-4-8 PE ISBN 978-0-9869495-1-7.

In 1975 Saigon, missionaries evacuated vulnerable disabled orphans who would be killed; Tuyet, eight, lame from polio, helps get over fifty tiny orphans flown to Canada, where she shows new caregivers how to comfort them. Skrypuch's third-person re-creation of these transitional months makes vivid the uncertainties of confronting a new language, climate, and family. Illustrated with photos. Reading list, websites. Ind.

Modern History; Disabilities, Physical; Vehicles–Airplanes; Canada; Orphans; History, Modern–Vietnam War; Vietnam; Diseases–Polio; Immigration; Missionaries

Skrypuch, Marsha Forchuk. One Step at a Time: A Vietnamese Child Finds Her Way. 104 pp. Pajama Press 2013. ISBN 978-1-927485-01-9 PE ISBN 978-1-927485-02-6.

This sequel to *Last Airlift* describes Tuyet's adjustment to life with her adoptive Canadian family, the drama this time revolving around the surgery she must have on her leg due to polio. Readers will be just as riveted to this quieter but no-less-moving story as Tuyet bravely dreams of being able to run and play. Illustrated with photos. Reading list, websites. Ind.

Individual Biographies; Disabilities, Physical; Vietnam; Adoption; Orphans; Surgery; Diseases–Polio; Immigration; Canada; Son Thi Anh, Tuyet

Smith, David J. If the World Were a Village: A Book About the World's People. 32 pp. Kids Can 2011. ISBN 978-1-55453-595-8 PE ISBN 978-0-7136-6880-3. Illustrated by Shelagh Armstrong. New ed., 2002.

304.6

This updated second edition asks readers to imagine "the whole population of the world as a village of just 100 people," with each person representing sixty-nine million people (it was sixty-two million in the previous edition). Smith covers topics such as nationalities, languages, food, etc. Accurately detailed acrylic art illustrates the thought-provoking book.

Social Issues; Economics; Population

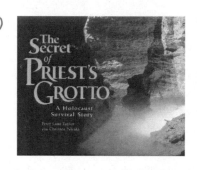

Taylor, Peter Lane and Nicola, Christos. The Secret of Priest's Grotto: A Holocaust Survival Story. 64 pp. Kar-Ben 2007. ISBN 978-1-58013-260-2 PE ISBN 978-1-58013-261-9

Caver Nicola learned that Jewish families hid in a Ukrainian cave during World War II. He and fellow caver/writer Taylor interviewed survivors, and this book presents their harrowing experience living underground for 344 days. Interwoven is the present-day account of Nicola and Taylor's 2003 expedition into the cave. Striking photographs help make the experience even more tangible for readers.

Modern History; Caves; History, Modern–Holocaust; Jews; Ukraine; Survival; Family

Taylor-Butler, Christine Sacred Mountain Everest. 48 pp. Lee 2009. ISBN 978-1-60060-255-9. This volume goes beyond the usual mountain-climbing focus to also explore the lives of Sherpas who make Everest their home. An introduction explains the mountain's local names and locates it on several maps. Subsequent chapters cover Sherpa customs, the mountain's flora and fauna, environmental concerns, and Everest explorations. Sidebars provide further information about people and geology. Well-reproduced photographs support the text. Timeline, websites. Bib., glos.

Middle East and Asia; Mountains and mountain life; Everest, Mount (China and Nepal)

J
943.155

Tunnell, Michael O. Candy Bomber: The Story of the Berlin Airlift's "Chocolate Pilot". 110 pp. Charlesbridge 2010. ISBN 978-1-58089-336-7 PE ISBN 978-1-58089-337-4.

American pilot Gail Halvorsen, along with his fellow servicemen, delivered candy to children in post-WWII West Berlin—dropping the treats from their bomber planes. Copious photographs and reproductions of letters bring the children's gratitude to life. By beginning with these personal stories, Tunnell piques readers' interest in learning more about the conflict between the Soviets and the Germans, information provided in later chapters. Reading list, websites. Bib., ind.

Europe; Vehicles–Airplanes; Pilots; United States Air Force; History, Modern–Cold War

Walker, Sally M. Blizzard of Glass: The Halifax Explosion of 1917. 141 pp. Holt 2011. ISBN 978-0-8050-8945-5 PE ISBN 978-1-250-04008-4.

In Halifax, on December 6, 1917, two ships collided in the harbor, one of them carrying an extraordinary amount of explosives. Walker sets the stage, then focuses on five families that lived in the waterfront neighborhoods. Through their eyes, we experience the explosion, devastating aftermath, and eventual rebuilding. Numerous black-and-white photographs, plus a couple of welcome maps, further chronicle events. Bib.

Modern History; Disasters; Vehicles–Ships; Canada; History, Modern–World War I

Wood, Douglas. Franklin and Winston: A Christmas That Changed the World. 40 pp. Candlewick 2011. ISBN 978-0-7636-3383-7. Illustrated by Barry Moser.

In December 1941, Winston Churchill spent the holidays with Franklin Roosevelt. They formed an alliance to fight the Axis Powers and crafted a charter for the United Nations. Wood's snapshot of this moment in history includes a few humorous anecdotes that add levity to an otherwise solemn text. Moser based his impressive watercolors on photographs from the period.

North America; Roosevelt, Franklin D.; Holidays–Christmas; Churchill, Winston; Presidents–United States; Prime ministers

–FOCUS ON–

THE HOLOCAUST

Rescue and Resistance

By Rachel Kamin

Rachel Kamin is the Director of the Joseph and Mae Gray Cultural & Learning Center at North Suburban Synagogue Beth El in Highland Park, IL.

MILTON MELTZER'S *Never to Forget* (HarperCollins, 1976) was one of the first children's books to explain the history of hatred that led to the Holocaust, the resultant process of destruction, and the courageous spirit of resistance. In *Rescue: The Story of How Gentiles Saved Jews in the Holocaust* (HarperCollins, 1988), Meltzer explains how he came "to realize the great importance of recording not just the evidence of evil, but also the evidence of human nobility." Students are exposed to this "human nobility" by reading about Righteous Gentiles, non-Jews who risked their lives to save Jews during the Holocaust. These stories, along with those of the Resistance and the nearly 10,000 children rescued in the Kindertransport, offer hope.

A study of this never-to-be-forgotten time in history calls for the deeper learning characterized by the Common Core State Standards. From picture-book biographies to fictional representations in books and film to documentary footage to archival documents and photographs, this materal can teach students to evaluate and understand perspective and content. Illustrated books introduce younger students to the topic while exploring drawings and photographs plays a critical role in adding to the meaning of a text. Older students can compare and contrast fictional portrayals of the Kindertransport in novels with the historical accounts found in informational titles. Add testimonies from the USC Shoah Foundation and students dig even deeper by analyzing multiple accounts of the same topic.

Most importantly, these stories of resistance, rescue, courage, ingenuity, and survival are a beacon of light amid the dark horrors of the Holocaust.

They inspire today's readers to live by Helmuth Hubener's words in *The Boy Who Dared* by Susan Campbell Bartoletti: "I don't want to remember a time I could have done something but didn't."

RIGHTEOUS GENTILES
Fiction

Bartoletti, Susan Campbell. The Boy Who Dared. Scholastic. 2008. Tr $16.99. ISBN 978-0-439-68013-4.
Gr 6-9–Helmuth Hubener, a German teen executed for treason and whom Bartoletti profiled in her *Hitler Youth* (Scholastic, 2005), is the main character in this fictionalized account. Imprisoned, Helmuth reflects on his crimes of listening to foreign newscasts, creating and distributing pamphlets, and committing acts of resistance to the Nazi Party. Audio version available from Listening Library.

Clark, Kathy. Guardian Angel House. (Holocaust Remembrance Series for Young Readers). Second Story. 2009. pap. $14.95. ISBN 978-1-897187-58-6.
Gr 4-7–Based on the experiences of her mother and aunt, Clark provides a compelling, fictionalized account documenting the courage and compassion of a group of nuns in Budapest who saved more than 100 Jewish children. Miraculously, the sisters are reunited with their parents through the aid of Raoul Wallenberg. Augmented with black-and-white photographs.

Deedy, Carmen Agra. The Yellow Star: The Legend of King Christian X of Denmark. illus. by Henri Sørensen. Peachtree. 2000. Tr $16.95. ISBN 978-1-56145-208-8.
Gr 3-5–Although no documented proof exists to support the legend of the king riding through the streets of Copenhagen with a yellow star sewn on his coat, the lyrical prose and dramatic full-page paintings make for an inspiring picture book and a powerful introduction to the remarkable story of the Jews of Denmark during World War II.

Nonfiction

Borden, Louise. His Name Was Raoul Wallenberg: Courage, Rescue, and Mystery During World War II. Houghton Harcourt. 2012. Tr $18.99. ISBN 978-0-618-50755-9.
Gr 5-8–Similar in format to Borden's *The Journey That Saved Curious George: The True Wartime Escape of Margret and H.A. Rey* (Houghton Harcourt, 2005), this book pairs photographs, documents, maps, and drawings with simple descriptive prose to retell the inspirational story of the Swedish diplomat who saved thousands of Jewish

citizens in Budapest. Wallenberg's life is also explored in the award-winning movie *Wallenberg: A Hero's Story* reissued by Paramount in 2011.

Meltzer, Milton. Rescue: The Story of How Gentiles Saved Jews in the Holocaust. HarperCollins. 1988. Tr $16.99. ISBN 978-0-06-024209-1; pap. $9.99. ISBN 978-0-06-446117-7.
Gr 6-10–Meltzer tells the stories of non-Jews, such as Oskar Schindler, Raoul Wallenberg, the people of Le Chambon, and the citizens of Denmark, who risked their lives to hide, smuggle, and feed Jews throughout Europe. Organized by country, each chapter includes a detailed map and historical information along with first-person testimonies, memoirs, diaries, oral histories, and letters.

Mochizuki, Ken. Passage to Freedom: The Sugihara Story. illus. by Dom Lee. Lee & Low. 1997. RTE $15.95. ISBN 978-1-880-00049-6; pap. $8.95. ISBN 978-1-584-30157-8.
Gr 3-5–When Jewish refugees lined up at the door of the Japanese consul to Lithuania, Chiune Sugihara chose to help more than 6000 people escape the Nazis. Illustrated with dark, sepia-toned illustrations, the story is told from the perspective of Sugihara's five-year-old son. Audio version available from Live Oak Media. The docudrama *The Visas That Saved Lives* (Marty Gross Film Productions, 2010) re-creates Sugihara's efforts.

Vaughan, Marcia. Irena's Jars of Secrets. illus. by Ron Mazellan. Lee & Low. 2011. RTE $18.95. ISBN 978-1-60060-439-3.
Gr 3-6–Irena Sendler, a young Catholic social worker, helped hundreds of Jews by smuggling food, clothing, and medicine into the Warsaw Ghetto and saved more than 2,500 children by smuggling them out of the ghetto to convents, orphanages, and Polish foster parents. Somber, double-spread illustrations rendered in oil on canvas add drama and emotion to the text.

JEWISH RESISTANCE
Fiction

Friedman, D. Dina. Escaping into the Night. S & S. 2009. Tr $17.99. ISBN 978-1-416-90258-4; pap. 8.99. ISBN 978-1-416-98648-5; ebook $8.99. ISBN 978-1-416-99665-1.
Gr 6-9–Based on the Bielski Brothers, a unit of partisans in the forests of western

Belorussia, this fictionalized account of a 13-year-old girl who escapes the ghetto and joins the resistance illuminates the story of the thousands of Jews who fought back. The PBS documentary *Resistance: Untold Stories of Jewish Partisans* (2008) includes rare archival footage and interviews with surviving partisans.

J
Fie

Hesse, Karen. The Cats in Krasinski Square. illus. by Wendy Watson. Scholastic. 2004. RTE $17.99. ISBN 978-0-439-43540-6.
Gr 3-5–With spare, powerful free-verse prose, Hesse tells the little-known story of how a group of young resistance fighters and stray cats outsmart the Gestapo at the Warsaw train station. Sensitive illustrations depict the sadness but not the horror of the time, making this an excellent read-aloud for younger students.

Meyer, Susan Lynn. Black Radishes. Delacorte. 2010. Tr $16.99. ISBN 978-0-385-73881-1; PLB $19.99. ISBN 978-0-385-90748-4; pap. $6.99. ISBN 978-0-375-85822-2; ebook $6.99. ISBN 978-0-375-89614-9.
Gr 5-8–Shortly before France is invaded by Germany, 11-year-old Gustave and his parents leave Paris for a small country village that luckily turns out to be south of the demarcation line. Along with his new friend Nicole, Gustave lends his hand to the French Resistance in this suspenseful tale.

Stuchner, Joan Betty. Honey Cake. illus. by Cynthia Nugent. Random. 2008. Tr $11.99. ISBN 978-0-375-85189-6; PLB $13.99. ISBN 978-0-375-95189-3; pap. $4.99. ISBN 978-0-375-85190-2; ebook $4.99. ISBN 978-0-307-47790-3.
Gr 3-5–David is only 10 years old when his father sends him out into the Nazi-occupied streets of Copenhagen with a box of chocolate éclairs to deliver to a friend. Unknowingly, David is carrying a secret message for the Danish Resistance. With soft pencil sketches, this is a gentle introduction to the period for transitional readers.

Nonfiction

Kacer, Kathy. The Underground Reporters. (Holocaust Remembrance Series). Second Story. 2003. pap. $15.95. ISBN 978-1-896764-85-6.
Gr 4-7–Alternating narratives interspersed with historical facts, photographs, maps, and drawings tell the story of an underground magazine created by a group of chil-

dren during the Nazi occupation. The book provides a detailed picture of what everyday life was like in Czechoslovakia and how the children's stories, poems, and drawings were a small, yet significant, form of resistance.

Rappaport, Doreen. Beyond Courage: The Untold Story of Jewish Resistance During the Holocaust. Candlewick. 2012. Tr $22.99. ISBN 978-0-7636-2976-2.
Gr 6 Up–Going beyond the well-known accounts of the Warsaw Ghetto Uprising and the escape from the Sobibor death camp, Rappaport retells 20 stories of defiance and resistance. The book is meticulously researched and masterfully organized, with archival photos and an accessible layout and design. Audio version available from Brilliance Audio.

HIDING TO SURVIVE
Fiction

Orlev, Uri. Run, Boy, Run. tr. from Hebrew by Hillel Halkin. Houghton Harcourt. 2003. Tr $16. ISBN 978-0-618-16465-3; pap. $6.95. ISBN 978-0-618-95706-4; ebook $6.95. ISBN 978-0-547-53099-4.
Gr 4-7–Full of action, adventure, and excitement, this novel tells the story of eight-year-old Srulik, who miraculously survived after being left alone in the Warsaw Ghetto. Orlev's *The Island on Bird Street* (Houghton Harcourt, 1984) also tells the story of a young survivor in the Ghetto and was made into a film of the same name (First Look Pictures, 2008).

Propp, Vera W. When the Soldiers Were Gone. Putnam. 2001. Tr $15. ISBN 978-1-422-35310-3; pap. $5.99. ISBN 978-0-698-11881-2.
Gr 3-6–Eight-year-old Henk learns, only when his Jewish parents come to claim him in 1945, that the couple he calls Mama and Papa are Dutch Christians who sheltered him on their farm during the war. Similar to Johanna Reiss's *The Upstairs Room* (HarperCollins, 1972), this is a gentler, yet no less dramatic, introduction to the subject for younger readers. Audio version available from Penguin Audio.

Roy, Jennifer. Yellow Star. Marshall Cavendish. 2006. Tr $16.95. ISBN 978-0-761-45277-5.
Gr 6-9–In 1939, 270,000 Jews were forced to move into the Lodz Ghetto. In 1945, there were only 800 survivors. Told in verse, the simple yet descriptive narrative relates the story of Syvia Perlmutter, the author's aunt and one of the 12 surviving children. Audio version available from Brilliance Audio.

Russo, Marisabina. I Will Come Back for You: A Family in Hiding During World War II. illus. by author. Random. 2011. Tr $17.99. ISBN 978-0-375-86695-1; PLB $20.99. ISBN 978-0-375-96695-8; ebook $10.99. ISBN 978-0-375-98515-7.

Gr 3-5–Nonna tells how her idyllic childhood in Rome ended abruptly when Italy joined the Germans. Papa is taken away, but Nonna, her brother, and mother escape to the countryside and survive the war hiding on a farm. Vivid gouache illustrations make this a gentle, hopeful introduction to the time period, much like the author's *Always Remember Me: How One Family Survived World War II* (Atheneum, 2005).

Nonfiction

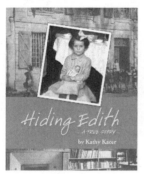

Kacer, Kathy. Hiding Edith: A True Story. (Holocaust Remembrance Series). Second Story. 2006. pap. $14.95. ISBN 978-1-897-18706-7.

Gr 4-6–After fleeing Vienna with her family, 12-year-old Edith was sheltered in a safe house for Jewish children in the town of Moissac, France. This retelling effectively combines the history of the war and hidden children with the specific experiences of an individual child. High-quality black-and-white photographs add appeal for student researchers and independent readers.

Mccann, Michelle R. & Luba Tryszynska-Frederick. Luba: The Angel of Bergen-Belsen. illus. by Ann Marshall. Tricycle. 2003. Tr $17.99. ISBN 978-1-582-46098-7.

Gr 3-5–With the women of her barracks, Luba Tryszynska-Frederick saved 52 Dutch children left in the forest to freeze by Nazi soldiers. Beautiful oil and collage illustrations depict Luba's life, her fellow inmates, and the children in Bergen-Belsen without displaying the horrors. Luba's story is featured in the 2008 History Channel anthology, *Heroes of the Holocaust: Tales of Resistance and Survival.*

Ruelle, Karen Gray & Deborah Durland DeSaix. The Grand Mosque of Paris: A Story of How Muslims Rescued Jews During the Holocaust. illus. by authors. Holiday House. 2009. RTE $18.95. ISBN 978-0-8234-2159-6; pap. $8.95. ISBN 978-0-8234-2304-0.

Gr 3-6–Beautiful full-spread oil paint illustrations, along with a detailed afterword, glossary, and bibliography, add to this unique tale of interfaith relations that relates the little-known story of Jews who were hidden by Muslims in the Grand Mosque of Paris during World War II.

Ruelle, Karen Gray & Deborah Durland DeSaix. Hidden on the Mountain: Stories of Children Sheltered from the Nazis in Le Chambon. Holiday House. 2007. Tr $24.95. ISBN 978-0-8234-1928-9.

Gr 6 Up–First-person accounts and black-and-white photos uncover the amazing story of the thousands of children who were sheltered in the tiny mountainous French village of Le Chambon-sur-Lignon. Fascinating and inspiring, this is a wonderful companion to the documentary *Weapons of the Spirit* (Chambon Foundation, 1989).

Taylor, Peter Lane with Christos Nicola. The Secret of Priest's Grotto: A Holocaust Survival Story. Kar-Ben. 2007. PLB $18.95. ISBN 978-1-58013-260-2; pap. $8.95. ISBN 978-1-58013-261-9.

Gr 6 Up–Full-color photographs and a compelling text reveal how 38 Jews endured with no training or special equipment for more than a year in the underground caves of the Western Ukraine. Readers also learn how their amazing story was discovered. The documentary *No Place on Earth* (Sierra Tango Productions, 2012) records the journey of four survivors back to the cave after more than 60 years.

RESCUED CHILDREN

Fiction

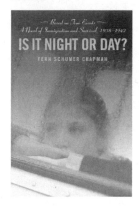

Chapman, Fern Schumer. Is It Night or Day? Farrar. 2010. Tr $16.99. ISBN 978-0-374-17744-7; ebook $9.99. ISBN 978-1-429-93413-8.

Gr 6-9–Using her mother's experiences as inspiration, Chapman delivers a moving account of Edith, a girl who travels to America with the assistance of One Thousand Children, an organization that rescued German children during the Holocaust. Edith's reunion, 70 years later, with the girl she befriended on her voyage, was profiled on the Oprah Winfrey Network's *Lost and Found* (January, 2013).

Taylor, Marilyn. Faraway Home. O'Brien Press. 2000. pap $12.95. ISBN 978-0-86278-643-4.

Gr 5-8–While most of the Jewish children on the Kindertransport were sent to Great Britain, a small minority traveled to Northern Ireland. This Irish import blends historical facts with fiction to tell the story of 13-year-old Karl, who is sent to work on a farm, and his younger sister, Rosa, who is taken in by a wealthy family.

○ **Thor, Annika.** A Faraway Island. tr. from Swedish by Linda Schenck. Delacorte. 2009. Tr $16.99. ISBN 978-0-385-73617-6; PLB $19.99. ISBN 978-0-385-90590-9; pap. $6.99. ISBN 978-0-375-84495-9; ebook $6.99. ISBN 978-0-375-89370-4.

Gr 5-8–In addition to the Kindertransport to Great Britain, 500 Jewish children were moved to safety in Sweden. This is the first in a series of novels about two sisters sent to a remote island near Göteborg. See also *The Lily Pond* (Delacorte, 2011); the third book, *Deep Sea*, is forthcoming. Audio version available from Listening Library.

○ **Watts, Irene.** Good-bye Marianne: A Story of Growing Up in Nazi Germany. Tundra. 2008. pap. $7.95. ISBN 978-0887764455; ebook $6.99. ISBN 978-1-77049-057-4.

Gr 4-7–Watts re-creates the first book of her trilogy that includes *Good-bye Marianne* (1998), *Remember Me* (2000), and *Finding Sophie* (2002) as a graphic novel. Based on her childhood in Berlin and her eventual move to England via the Kindertransport, this version is made more accessible to reluctant or less-proficient readers with simple yet expressive black-and-white pencil drawings.

Nonfiction

○

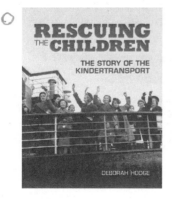

Hodge, Deborah. Rescuing the Children: The Story of the Kindertransport. Tundra. 2012. Tr $17.95. ISBN 978-1-77049-256-1; ebook $10.99. ISBN 978-1-77049-366-7.

Gr 4-7–In this succinct overview of the Kindertransport rescue operations that took almost 10,000 Jewish youngsters to Great Britain between December 1938 and the start of World War II, the stories of eight individual children are enhanced by photos, text boxes, quotes, drawings, maps, and a time line.

ON THE WEB

For Librarians and Teachers

For Teachers: Teaching About the Holocaust. www.ushmm.org/education/foreducators. United States Holocaust Memorial Museum. (Accessed 2/24/13).

This well-organized, comprehensive site houses a host of resources including online workshops, lesson plans, and discussion guides as well as videos, music, and personal histories.

Jewish Partisan Educational Foundation. jewishpartisans.org. Jewish Partisan Educational Foundation (JPEF). (Accessed 2/24/13).
RESIST, a curriculum designed by the JPEF to teach 6th–12th-grade students about Jewish partisans who fought the Nazis, includes study guides, lessons, and activities. The website also features an interactive map, a virtual underground bunker, short film clips, and a list of resources.

KTA: The Kindertransport Association. kindertransport.org. The Kindertransport Association. (Accessed 2/24/13).
Users will find an accessible history of the Kindertransport rescue movement that saved nearly 10,000 children from Nazi Germany, Austria, Poland, and Czechoslovakia. Includes photographs, documents, articles, online resources, and an extensive bibliography of books, films, and government documents.

For Students

The Righteous Among the Nations. www.yadvashem.org/yv/en/righteous/index.asp.
Yad Vashem. (Accessed 2/24/13).
Gr 6 Up–Maintained by Yad Vashem, "the Jewish people's living memorial to the Holocaust" in Jerusalem, this online resource features more than 100 rescue stories, including Irena Sendler, Oskar Schindler, Chiune Sugihara, and Raoul Wallenberg, with biographical articles, short video testimonies, documents, photos, and links to related information.

Eds. note: The full version of "Rescue and Resistance"
is available online at http://ow.ly/rnkNg

Title Index

Author/Illustrator Index